THE REIGN OF SATAN

Benjamin Gastineau (1823-1904), originally a typographer, was won over to Proudhon's ideas and became a journalist for the latter's *La Voix du Peuple*, which earned him a conviction in 1848. An opponent of the Bonapartist regime, he was expelled to Algeria in 1852. Returning to France, he established himself in Saint-Quentin and became editor-in-chief of the journal *Le Guetteur*, which, in 1858, was banned for inciting the working class against the established order. He was arrested once again and, once again, deported to Algeria. Granted amnesty in 1859, he continued his activities as a journalist in the provinces. With the fall of the Second Empire, he returned to Paris, where he joined the Commune and became involved in revolutionary newspapers and clubs. When the Commune fell, he escaped repression by fleeing to Belgium. He returned to France after the amnesty of 1880. He published a large number of books of both fiction and non-fiction, including *Le Carnaval* (1855) *Monsieur et Madame Satan* (1864), *P.-J. Proudhon, sa vie et son œuvre* (1865), and *H. Taine sa vie, son oeuvre philosophique et littéraire* (1867).

BENJAMIN GASTINEAU

THE REIGN OF SATAN
OR
THE RICH AND THE POOR

THIS IS A SNUGGLY BOOK

Copyright © 2021by Snuggly Books.
All rights reserved.

ISBN: 978-1-64525-067-8

This edition of *The Reign of Satan* is a reprint of that which was originally published in 1851. The translation, however, has been significantly revised.

THE REIGN OF SATAN

I.

THE HIGH ROAD

ONE cold January morning, a woman, bearing a child in her arms, was to be seen passing quickly along the road that leads from Ambroise to the village of Vouvray; her ragged clothes and haggard looks announced great suffering; the path, rendered hard and uneven by the freezing of the mud, lacerated her feet. From time to time, her look dived into the lengthy space before her, as if she wished to measure the extent of way she had yet to go before arriving at her destination. Then she would bend her head downwards, in order to increase, with her breath, the warmth of the child she was carrying. A thick fog hid the sun, and cast on everything around that grey and gloomy aspect which saddens the sight, and inspires melancholy. The dead silence of the way was only broken by the passage of some bird, seeking a refuge from the cold. Like the poor pedestrian, nature was dumb and desolate. Presently, Magdalene Simon uttered a faint cry; she had just perceived the village where she hoped to find an end to her suffering. Strengthened by this sight, she doubled her speed; but she had scarcely passed the first two or three houses in Vouvray, when she stopped irresolute before the gate of a farm-house. At length, casting her eyes, filled with tears, towards heaven, she held forth her hands, as if imploring protection for her infant, and then, with an uncertain step, entered the yard. A farm-boy came to meet her. She asked to see Mr. Simon.

"He's up the orchard," replied Nicholas. "I'll go and fetch him. Your name, if you please?"

Magdalene appeared embarrassed at this demand.

"My name," said she, "my name—oh, never mind—it's useless. Tell Mr. Simon that a woman wishes to speak to him."

Nicholas ran to tell his master, and Magdalene entered a large room that opened on the yard. An immense wood fire blazed on the hearth; after having approached it, Magdalene, visibly affected, looked around. In every object she perceived a souvenir. How often had her mother nursed her before that fire-place! from that window she had seen *him* for the first time! While thinking of her happy childhood, Magdalene fell into a reverie, which might have been called a disappearance of the present and a reappearance of the past. Such reveries are ever dear to the unfortunate, who are thus sometimes enabled to deceive the reality, and, for a moment, to forget all their trouble, by carrying their thoughts back to an epoch when no adverse wind had as yet ruffled the calm, clear stream of their happiness. Farmer Simon, followed by his son Jacques, soon entered the room. He was a man of about fifty, of commanding stature, to whom long, red hair, very thick eyebrows, a bony face, and small eyes, gave a look of cunning and harshness. He did not recognise Magdalene.

"What's your business?" said he, bluntly, advancing towards her. Magdalene was about to throw her arms round her father's neck, but the recollection of her actual situation flashed across her mind, and she fell on her knees. "Father," said she, "don't you then know your daughter?"

"I have no longer a daughter," replied the father, when recovered from his surprise.

"Pity! have pity on me, father!" sobbed Magdalene, clasping Simon's knees, and endeavouring to kiss his hands.

The farmer violently pushed her from him.

"What!' said he, in a voice trembling with rage, "you dare, after all that has taken place, present yourself before me? Leave—leave instantly,—out of my house, with my curse upon you!"

"Oh! father," sobbed Magdalene, "you cannot mean thus to drive away your daughter, whom repentance brings to your feet! Father, I have already been punished for my faults; severely have I expiated them! Oh, why—why did I not become the wife of Matthias, according to your wish!"

"Because," replied Simon, "you preferred decamping with the wretch to whom you forfeited your honour."

"If I had remained," sobbed Magdalene, "you would have killed me; and then I loved him—loved him to distraction!"

Any other man save Simon would have been touched by this painful avowal; but, insensible to his daughter's despair, he replied, in a tone of irony:—

"And so you sacrificed your own honour, as well as that of your family, to a vile seducer, who, no doubt, worthily returned your love—eh?"

"You shall judge," replied Magdalene. "When she, whom he had led astray, by promising eternal love, became a mother, he turned her, without pity, from his house. He threw her on this wide world, without a farthing. But you will not imitate him, will you, father? Pity! oh, pity! Let me again come home. From morning to night I will try, by care and attention, to repair the harm I have done you. And some day, perhaps, when you see that my heart harbours love but for one person—for my father only—you will forget my past faults, and again look upon me as your daughter. O, let me hope this day will come!"

"Never!" exclaimed the infuriated farmer. "The wretched creature who has dishonoured my name shall never again shelter her guilty head under my roof."

"I am penniless," replied Magdalene; "I have sought for work; I have wished to go to service; but I have everywhere met with a refusal, on account of my child. In the whole world there is but you to whom I can apply. If you abandon me, what will become of me—whither can I go?"

"Where you please. She who has committed the crime must suffer the punishment," growled Simon.

"In the name of my mother, I implore you to receive me!" cried Magdalene.

"Speak not of your mother; it is you who have killed her, wretch!" answered her father.

"Jacques!" said Magdalene, in despair, turning towards her brother, who had hitherto been a silent spectator of this painful scene, "will you also abandon me?"

"I must obey father," drily replied the farmer's son.

"Then I'll beg no more, father," said Magdalene. "I know my fault is too great in your eyes, to be diminished or expiated by repentance or tears. I have deserved your anger; but oh, do not also visit it on the head of my poor, starving, innocent babe. Protect him at least; I will then go—go to—you shall never, never see me again. Heaven will reward you for this action. You will save a life; for if my son remains with me, he will die."

It was in vain that Magdalene tried to soften her father; tears and prayers were alike useless. Simon, like many more, had never felt his heart beat within his breast. While his daughter in tears demanded pardon, he, hardly able to restrain his passion, motioned her with his extended finger towards the door.

"If you do not leave directly," cried he, after his daughter's last appeal, "I'll not answer for the consequences!"

"In pity for my child!" again cried Magdalene.

"Your child! your child!" replied the farmer, furiously; "take him with you, or, perdition seize him, for these flames shall instantly devour the fruit of your crime!"

Simon accompanied this diabolical threat with a horrid gesture, and Magdalene, uttering a piercing cry, snatched her child up in her arms.

The imprecations of the father had completely metamorphosed the daughter; she no longer supplicated; her attitude became firm and imposing. In his turn, Simon felt influenced by a power superior to his own.

"Silence! silence!" said Magdalene, horrified. "You are no longer my father; I disown you. To menace my child! Oh! no, you cannot be my father, you cannot! The only father I now have is in heaven, whence He sees and judges me; He alone can save me. I want nothing more. Adieu! adieu!"

She quitted the room, leaving Simon and his son stupified with this sudden transformation.

The farmer's menace, the most terrible that a mother could hear, had made Magdalene forget both cold and hunger. She ran like a maniac through the village, her father's words still ringing in her ears. As soon as she had become somewhat calm, the thought recurred to her mind, "How shall I find protection for my child?" There was but one alternative: to knock at a cottage door, and ask for charity. Unfortunately, a peasant had recognised her, as she entered Vouvray. The whole village had been directly made acquainted with her arrival. Discussions immediately arose as to whether her father would take her in or not. Animated by that low curiosity, so greedy of scandal, and which seems inherent to people inhabiting small places, the peasants had assembled in groups before their doors, to talk about this *grave* event. Magdalene perceived that she was the object of their attention. Their words even reached her, by which she was soon made acquainted with the opinion held of her by the good people of Vouvray.

"That's my lady; that's Simon's daughter," said one.

"Yes," replied another; "Magdalene Simon, who ran away, one fine morning, with the son of the squire's steward; it's two years ago, come Midsummer. It doesn't appear that she has made her fortune at Paris."

"No," said another, "it seems that all she has brought back with her is a young's un."

"So much the worse for her. She might have expected it."

"It just serves her right."

They all cried out together: "She has got what she deserves!"

The anguish which these words caused Magdalene was excessive. She staggered, while passing those groups of persons who were cowardly insulting her, and laughing at her fate; her heart was ready to burst. Her grief having attained, at last, its highest degree of intensity, she fell into so complete a state of mental prostration, that she lost the sentiment even of her very existence.

The protecting hand of Providence has imposed a limit to grief as well as to joy. This limit once passed, the faculties of man become diminished, and his reason wanders. Poignant grief leads to a callous state of feeling, and excessive joy to intoxication. As soon as Magdalene was able to throw off this despondency, her first thought was again given to her child. She had still a hope—the hope of finding a place containing people more compassionate.

"From Vouvray to Saint-George," said she, "it is but six miles. By walking fast, I shall be able to arrive there tonight; my child must not perish."

Magdalene's efforts to triumph over her lassitude and exhaustion were almost superhuman, but, alas! she was doomed to succumb. Night overtook her; the cold became more intense. She began to feel symptoms of fever. Her limbs shivered, and a cold sweat inundated her temples. Attributing this to fatigue, she sat down on a little mound. After having rested herself for a few moments, she again commenced her way; she had scarcely risen, however, when she fell heavily to the ground near the place she had just quitted. Suffering had exhausted her strength and destroyed all her energy. But the thought that death might overtake her while thus alone with her infant, gave fresh strength to her in her despair; and she cried aloud for help in the most piercing tones of distress.

Her voice, carried away by the wind, was lost in space, and no being replied to her appeal: she tried again to rise: it was useless. She felt as though she were rooted to the ground. In her despair, she had but the strength to weep, and her tears were frozen as they fell.

"Oh, Heaven! oh, Heaven!" murmured the wretched mother, "my boy must not die here: it would be too frightful!"

At this moment two objects that looked like balls of fire were seen upon the road. An equipage was advancing towards her at a rapid rate.

"Thank Heaven!" said she, "my prayer has been heard—my son will yet be saved!"

Magdalene crawled to the roadside, at the risk of being crushed to pieces by the horses or the wheels; and, as the coach passed, she cried, with all the energy of her distress and agony:—

"A child and a woman are dying here! come to their help."

Her cry was heard.

The coachman, who possessed some humanity, suddenly stopped his horses. But a head, enveloped in handkerchiefs, was immediately thrust out of the window, and a voice vociferated:—

"Who ordered you to stop here, you ass?—on!"

At the sound of that voice, Magdalene uttered a shriek, and fell back, fainting. The head enveloped in handkerchiefs disappeared; the coachman lashed his horses into a gallop, and the carriage was quickly whirled away. Luckily, a traveller had heard her piercing cry of distress, and ran to her assistance. Little by little Magdalene recovered her consciousness; but her respiration was short and painful. The breath of life was fast quitting her: so many emotions had worn her out.

"Maurice—my child," she murmured faintly.

"He is here," said the stranger.

"In—the carriage—that has just passed," gasped Magdalene, "is the father of my child—oh! infamy! I am dying!—How I suffer! Death so near, and no one to save my child!"

"How shall I procure assistance for her?" said the stranger.

"Oh, who will take care of my child—my child?" asked Magdalene, in death's whisper.

"I—I will, poor young mother," said the stranger. "Your prayer shall be heard: I will bring up your son: from this day, he shall become my own."

"Oh! thank you, thank you," convulsively replied the dying mother.

"May this promise prove a consolation to you in your last moments," added the stranger, "and render less painful your eternal adieu to this world, where, forsaken by all, you seem to have met with nothing but shame and misery. God, however, has kept an account of each torture of your heart: you will be able, from heaven, to watch over your child, whom I henceforth adopt, and whom I will never abandon."

"Oh! blessings—blessings on you—whoever you be, I——"

The words expired on her lips. Another convulsion, and she breathed her last. The stranger gently laid her body in the ditch by the roadside. This done, he came back to quiet Maurice, who was crying for his mother.

"Your mother will answer you no more, my child," said he; "she is now in heaven."

The stranger then took his cloak, wrapped it warmly round the child, and continued his journey.

In a few minutes, the snow, which fell in large flakes, had formed a winding-sheet round Magdalene's body.

II.

A DISCIPLE OF VINCENT DE PAULE

THE person who had so generously undertaken to protect Magdalene's child, was named Jérôme Ballue, and exercised, at Saint-George, a pretty village on the north side of the Loire, a profession as honourable as it is unprofitable,—that of schoolmaster.

Society often honours its members in direct opposition to the services they render it. The most useful and honourable men are often the most unfortunate; this circumstances suffices to qualify our judgement of it.

The present was not the first time that Jérôme Ballue had given proof of possessing the heart of a Vincent de Paule.

The following recital will more fully make known his character:—

In 1816, during the holidays, family affairs had forced him to go to Paris with his wife Catherine.

The evening before their departure from the capital, they heard, while passing before a church, the cries of a child. Jérôme left his wife, and ran immediately to the church door. In a corner, at the top of the steps, he perceived a small basket, of which he took possession.

"There, Catherine, that's what I've found," said he, presenting the basket to his wife.

By the light of a lamp, Catherine saw a little innocent babe, that stretched its tiny arms towards her. A medallion hung from its neck. It was the portrait, doubtless, of the infant's mother.

"Well, what must we do with it?" said Jérôme, looking at his wife.

"Why, Jérôme," she replied, "I think we must accept what Heaven has sent us, and take care of the little creature."

"Catherine," replied her husband, "you are the pearl of women."

The next day they quitted Paris, taking with them the little girl that they had found on the steps of St. Roch's. When they reached their home, they christened her Juliette.

This good deed did not preserve Jérôme from misfortune. His good Catherine died prematurely, and the schoolmaster, was left alone with his adopted child. His salary, as schoolmaster, was about 800 francs a year. By singing at church on Sundays, he raised it, however, to 1,000: a small sum for two beings to exist upon.

At the time our story commences, Jérôme Ballue was fifty-two; his body, which was extremely thin, and his bony face, announced long privation. The spark of life seemed to have taken refuge in his eyes, which were as bright and ardent as the last embers of a furnace. Though living in great poverty, a complaint never passed the lips of the village schoolmaster: he hid all physical suffering in the joys of the soul. The sight of his little family, as he designated his scholars, rendered him happy.

Jérôme did not content himself with teaching the children to read; he attended perseveringly to their moral education, in the improvement of which he spared neither time nor patience. His method was as simple as it was successful. It consisted of maintaining in the minds of his pupils the superiority of good instincts over bad ones. He looked upon childhood as a field in which both good and bad herbs grow abundantly; and upon the schoolmaster as an agriculturalist, whose duty it is to destroy the tares that choke the golden crop in its growth.

At dinner, for example, when he remarked one of his pupils making his meals off dry bread, he approached another, who was more lucky, and whispered to him:—

"Look at poor little Pierre, how sad he looks, dining off dry bread!"

The child thus addressed would immediately run and divide his little dainties with his less fortunate schoolfellow.

When his pupils had finished, Jérôme would return to his room and partake of his own meal, which, very, very often consisted of nothing but bread and water. As soon as his repast was over, he used to place himself at a window which looked into the yard where his scholars were playing: his eye would then dilate, his face expand, and every feature betray an expression of the most indescribable joy.

As he looked upon them, and heard them shouting, frolicking, and revelling in the happiness of their young hearts, "Oh, why," he would say, "must they some day quit me? How lovely they look now! What will the world do with them by and bye? I shall send them into it good and happy; it will make them wicked and miserable. At present they are united by love; a few years more, and hatred will tear them from each other: hatred, the fruit of selfishness, envy, and presumption. May they, at least, in the midst of their after-struggles and contentions, keep the recollection of old Jérôme and the school at Saint-George, where they lived as brothers, and formed but one family! and may the Almighty, who inspires them with love today, defend them from hatred ever after! But, why must they leave me?"

The two orphans, Maurice and Juliette, grew up under the vigilant eye of Jérôme, whose paternal instructions they willingly attended to.

Juliette had attained her fifteenth year. She was a fair, delicate girl. Her features, around which her golden hair fell in flowing streams, were stamped with that expression of purity which Raphael so much loved to give to his female faces. Good, obliging, and charitable, she had gained the affections of all who knew her.

Maurice, as good and sensible, and nearly of the same age as Juliette, differed from her materially in character. Juliette was gay and communicative, Maurice sombre and reserved. The gravity of the youth drew now and then a sly, laughing sarcasm from Juliette, but it was in vain that she tried to dispel his sadness. The image of his mother, expiring on the roadside, had stamped itself on his mind, and was always sure to come and place itself between him and any amusement circumstances might offer. Her phantom appeared before him in many a sleepless night. In fact, this terrible apparition was continually present to his mind. Jérôme tried to drive it from his pupil's thoughts, but unsuccessfully. Every day, Maurice said to him: "Oh! tell me something more about my mother." Yet he knew that he could but hear what he had already heard a thousand times.

Maurice was passionately fond of study. He early evinced great taste for drawing. Without any other master but his own inclination, he soon drew very skilfully. His vocation was revealed in rather a strange manner. One day, at church, his eyes fell on a picture, the subject of which was the *Flight into Egypt*. Maurice had already seen this picture, but never before had it produced on him the impression he then felt. The face of the Virgin had never before appeared to him so pure, so exquisitely beautiful. It seemed as if the figures painted on the canvass were animated by life, and were smiling on him.

The youth, carried into ideal regions, did not perceive that everyone had left the church. Jérôme was obliged to come and put an end to his ecstasy.

"Come, Maurice," he said, touching him on the shoulder, "don't you see that everyone has left?"

"Father," replied Maurice, "I must be a painter."

"A painter?" exclaimed the poor schoolmaster, astonished.

"Yes, father," answered Maurice.

"But to become a painter," said Jérôme, "don't you know that you want both time and—money?"

"Ah, yes," said Maurice, with a sigh, "true; excuse me, father. This picture had made me forget that."

"Don't despair, though," said Jérôme; "in your leisure time you shall study drawing, your favourite occupation. Every man, Maurice, ought to follow, as much as possible, the vocation for which his ideas and taste give him an inclination. He who, from predilection, fulfils the humblest functions, however much despised, is happy."

Maurice profited by this encouragement. All his leisure time was henceforth occupied in drawing. Unfortunately, an unexpected event took place which altered all his projects.

One Sunday he returned home, with a bleeding face, and his clothes in disorder. As soon as Jérôme perceived him, he cried out:—

"Why, what's the matter, Maurice?"

"I've been fighting," was the reply.

"Fighting! what about?" exclaimed Jérôme.

"Because they insulted my mother's memory," answered the youth.

"And who dared do so?"

"A boy of the name of Matthias."

"How could he know who you were? They all think that I found you abandoned on the highroad; no one knows the name of your mother, nor her unfortunate fate."

"Everyone knows it now," sobbed Maurice.

"Come, tell me everything," said the schoolmaster, kindly.

"While I was going by the church," began Maurice, "I saw Matthias and a great many more pointing and laughing at me. As I approached, I heard them say: 'Oh, yes, it's he; it's the son of—' oh! no, I can never repeat their insulting words. I was not able to contain myself; so I ran towards Matthias, called him a liar and a coward, and then rushed on him like a madman. My indignation doubled my strength; I threw him down, and I think I should have killed him, had they not rescued him from me. My poor mother suffered enough during her life, without being calumniated after her death."

"Come, Maurice, calm yourself," said Jérôme, soothingly. "Matthias merits nothing but your disdain. I will take care to stop his calumnies."

"What have I done to have my mother's memory insulted?" sobbed Maurice. "I have never shown them anything but kindness."

At this moment, Juliette was heard coming downstairs, humming a lively tune.

"I'll go out for an instant, father; I should betray myself if I remained," replied Maurice. And shaking Jérôme by the hand, he glided out of the house.

Maurice's anger was not of long duration; little by little, it dwindled away, and was succeeded by sad and melancholy thoughts. As he was walking through the village, a piercing cry suddenly fell upon his ear. He looked up, and perceived a horse, dragging after it, at a furious rate, a tilbury, which was every instant threatened to be dashed to pieces, and a woman, bent half-way out of the vehicle, was imploring assistance.

At this sight, Maurice, listening but to the first impulse of his generous nature, and without once thinking of the danger, immediately rushed to the horse's head, and, clinging to the reins, gave them a violent jerk. The animal having plunged a good deal, stopped a few paces further on; but the courageous Maurice was knocked down and trodden under foot. A young girl alighted from the tilbury; as soon as she had recovered from her fright, she inquired after her preserver.

"What!" cried she, "he is wounded! wounded! oh, heaven!" She immediately ran to Maurice, who was lying senseless in the middle of the road, threw back from his forehead his black hair, now saturated with blood, and held to him a small bottle of smelling salts, which she took from her pocket.

When Maurice was come to himself, they carried him home; and a surgeon was sent for. He said that Maurice's wounds, though extremely bad, would not, however, endanger his life.

The young lady, forgetting, in her solicitude for her preserver, the constraint imposed on her sex, remained at the head of his bed, bestowing, in concert with Juliette, all the care and attention that his state required. When her carriage was announced, she sent word that it would not be wanted before nine o'clock the next morning.

"What, Madam," said Juliette, timidly, "is it your intention to remain all night with——?"

"With your brother?" continued the lady. "Yes."

"But, Madam, such kindness—"

"Is much too little," replied the lady, interrupting Juliette.

"But I shall not leave him. He will be well nursed, I assure you," said Juliette.

"I do not doubt it," continued the lady; "but if you were to leave now, I should carry with me the greatest uneasiness. I cannot leave this house until I have the certitude that your brother is out of danger."

"How kind you are! I shall ever love you!" exclaimed Juliette.

Thus, these two young girls, like guardian angels, watched at the bedside of the patient. Maurice passed an agitated night. The next morning, when he opened his eyes, he saw, by the side of his bed, a young creature, whose almost angelic beauty made him think for a moment that it was a vision. He remained for an instant absorbed in contemplation. Wishing, however, to know whether he were under the influence of a dream, he said, gently: "I feel very thirsty."

The young lady immediately rose, took a cup, containing some soothing mixture, and gave it to him.

"Who are you?" said Maurice, trying to collect his thoughts.

"Your friend," replied his fair nurse; "she whom, yesterday, you saved from death. My name is Lucie Delaborde, niece of Mr. Jacques Delaborde, the well-known merchant of Tours. Do not forget," added she, with a look of gratitude, "that I shall esteem the day, on which you give me an opportunity of providing my gratitude, the happiest of my life. In the meantime, I can only thank you."

"'Tis I, Madam," replied Maurice, "who thank heaven for having allowed me to save one of its angels."

At nine o'clock, Lucie bid goodbye to Jérôme and his family. Two months afterwards, after having packed up his things, he said to Jérôme: "Father, I am going to leave you."

"Leave me! what do you mean?" stammered the poor schoolmaster.

"I am going to Tours—I must go," replied Maurice.

"Is that how you ask for my permission?" said Jérôme, his eyes filled with tears.

"Father," continued Maurice, "you little know how much it costs me to leave you and my sister. But I cannot remain at St. George, after what has taken place. Then, at my age, I ought to be earning my own living. I'm ashamed of being still a burden on you; I know you undergo many privations for my sake. It is on this account also that I have resolved to go to Tours. Miss Delaborde will procure me work in her uncle's manufactory."

"Since your resolution is taken, I will not try to dissuade you. But who has put this idea into your head?" asked the poor schoolmaster.

"My mother, whom I saw in a dream," replied Maurice.

"May Heaven protect you, my child, and—" At this moment Juliette entered to wish her father good morning.

"Embrace me also, Juliette," said Maurice.

"Willingly," she replied, throwing her arms round her brother's neck.

"This is our parting kiss," added he.

"What! Maurice, are you going to leave us?" asked Juliette.

"For a short time. It is necessary: is it not, father?" said Maurice.

The schoolmaster gave no answer. He turned away to hide his tears.

"Goodbye, father! adieu, Juliette!"

A quarter of an hour afterwards Maurice was on his way to Tours.

There was not much done that day in the school-room at Saint George. After Jérôme and his daughter had watched Maurice till he could be no longer seen, they entered the house again, dispirited and sad; and when night fell, they were both still grieving.

III.

THE MANUFACTURER

IN 1832, trade was in a flourishing condition in Tours. Mr. Jacques Delaborde was at that time the leading manufacturer of the town. He was the proprietor of a cloth manufactory, and employed above two hundred workmen. The factory was an immense building of five stories; each story forming a long room, in which several powerful engines, worked by steam, were in continual motion.

The manufacturer himself rarely visited his workshops. Being a philanthropist, how could he? The sight of his wretched workmen, enervated by toil and misery—that sacrilegious union, that scourge of the people—would have been too much for him. He resided in a charming villa, at little more than a stone's throw from the town.

There are some beings who struggle all their lives against an untoward destiny, without ever triumphing over it: there are, on the contrary, others who never meet with an obstacle. Among this latter class might be placed Jacques Delaborde. The son of a poor farmer, he determined to be rich, and his mind was entirely absorbed by this one idea. Chance favoured him; he speculated boldly with a small capital, and in a few years was the possessor of an immense fortune. He had longed for riches, and had obtained them: that is his whole history. At the moment we introduce him to our readers, he was seated in his private room, with a person already known to them, Miss Lucie Delaborde. The bald head, flat nose, and ruddy comlexion of the manufacturer formed a striking contrast with the classic beauty of his niece.

Lucie was in her eighteenth year. Owing to a precocious nature, inherited from her mother, who was Italian, her body and mind had already attained their entire development. Her features were full of intelligence, life, and earnestness. Her soft blue eyes were surmounted by dark eyebrows, beautifully formed; and a sonorous voice denoted the firmness of her character. In her beauty were united those extremely opposite gifts, firmness and grace.

The manufacturer, generally gay, was now knitting his brows, and trying to look as magisterial as possible.

"Lucie," said he to his niece, "I have a serious matter to talk to you about.

"Good gracious, uncle!" replied Lucie, frightened by his unusually measured tone, "has any accident happened?"

"On the contrary, I think that you will leave this room more pleased than you were, when you entered it," replied Mr. Delaborde.

"In that case, uncle, make haste, I beg of you," said Lucie.

"Lucie," began Mr. Delaborde, and he put his hand into his bosom and half shut his eyes, "Lucie, at eight years of age, you lost your father. Your mother, you know, was greatly attached to him; so much so, that, two years afterwards, she followed him to the grave. At ten, you were an orphan."

"Why do you call this to my mind, uncle?" said Lucie, her eyes filling with tears.

"My sister-in-law," continued the manufacturer, without noticing the interruption, "left you two hundred thousand francs, appointed me your guardian, and I promised, at her death-bed, to watch over the happiness of her child."

"Oh! you have nobly kept your promise," sobbed Lucie: "my gratitude will be eternal."

"You must not interrupt me."

"Excuse me; it was involuntary," said Lucie.

"My sister-in-law," continued Mr. Delaborde, with still greater gravity, "wished you to be brought up by her friend, Miss Lebrun, of Paris. I sent you to her, and your education is now finished; but you have yet to fulfil your mother's last wish."

"Oh! let me know it," exclaimed Lucie, with a palpitating heart; "oh! with what pleasure will I obey her! 'Tis a sacred duty."

"Lucie, you are now more than eighteen," again began Mr. Delaborde.

"Yes, uncle, I was eighteen last May," added Lucie.

"It is time, then, for you to begin to think of your future happiness," said her uncle, still maintaining his look of solemnity.

Lucie, on hearing this, could not suppress a feeling of uneasiness.

"I wish for nothing," she stammered; "I am very happy here with you."

"But if you desire, Miss Delaborde, to fulfil your mother's last wish, it will be necessary for you to become the wife of my son Albert," said the manufacturer.

A complete silence followed. Lucie, thunderstruck, could not utter a single word.

"I am certain," continued Mr. Delaborde, who was a very bad observer of human nature, "that this union will prove agreeable to you. My son is an accomplished, gentlemanly young man. Many a young lady will envy you such a husband."

While her uncle was speaking, Lucie had become frightfully pale. Horror and fear were depicted on her countenance.

"Oh! uncle," said she, "you have made me very unhappy."

"Unhappy!" exclaimed Mr. Delaborde, astounded, "unhappy! and why?"

"Because it will be impossible for me to comply with my mother's wish," said Lucie.

"Impossible!" echoed her uncle.

"Is not marriage, uncle, a bond which unites two persons, drawn towards each other by mutual sympathy?" asked Lucie.

"Undoubtedly," replied the manufacturer, disconcerted by this sentimental theory of marriage.

"In that case, I must tell you that I do not love my cousin Albert," replied Lucie.

"Oh! is that all?" exclaimed her uncle, bursting into a horse-laugh. "The obstacle is not great. Albert has been playing you some trick, perhaps. He is so full of spirits! But he has repented already; and, besides, you must forget these things."

"You told me, uncle," remarked Lucie, solemnly, "that you wished to speak seriously with me: I must beg you to think that the answer I have given you is serious." This was said with so much dignity and resolution, that Mr. Delaborde appeared vexed and astonished.

"How," asked he, "was your time occupied at school, Miss Delaborde, for you to be ignorant that the first duty of a daughter is to obey her parents?

I shall certainly see that your mother's wish be fulfilled."

"My mother," replied Lucie, without being in the least disconcerted, "though she might desire to see me married to my cousin would never, I am sure, have forced my inclination. If she were still living, I should tell her, as I now tell you, that, were I to become my cousin's wife, my happiness would be destroyed forever. And she, far from esteeming me disobedient, would approve of my refusal."

Mr. Delaborde, beaten in argument by the firm, good sense of his niece, was fain to continue the conversation in a tone of playfulness.

"Lucie," said he, "I should be angry, did I imagine that your aversion for your cousin proceeded from anything but momentary ill-humour. But here is the culprit himself," added Mr. Delaborde, pointing to his son, who had just entered the room: "I shall make him atone in my presence.

"You come very *à propos*," said Mr. Delaborde to his son. "Come and ask your cousin's forgiveness for your sins, Sir."

"If to love passionately is to be guilty," replied Albert, leering presumptuously at Lucie, "I own to having sinned."

"And uselessly," answered Miss Delaborde, "for your love never has been, and never will be, returned."

"My cousin is difficult to please," replied Albert, waspishly, and with a face purple from rage.

"Certainly, though," continued he, "when people possess every good quality and every virtue, they have the right to expect the like perfection in others."

"Come, come," interrupted Mr. Delaborde; "you do not go the right way to obtain your pardon. You are both spoilt children. You know, Albert, that your marriage with Lucie is fixed for this day month. So, my boy, make good use of your time. I shall leave you now, in order that you may be able to speak more freely together. There, make it up."

After this advice, the manufacturer left the room, laughing boisterously, but yet sick at heart.

"Why, what have I done Lucie?" exclaimed Albert, in a conciliating tone, and drawing near his cousin. "Will you always reply to the sincerity of my affection by unmerited disdain? I ought to hate you, for you seize every opportunity of speaking ill of me. Yet I do not; I have not the courage to do so. I adore my beautiful enemy to such a degree, that I would willingly give my life to obtain from her a look without anger, or a word without reproach."

"Well, this is delightful!" said Lucie, falling into a bit of laughter. "Oh, admirable! the height of romance and gallantry!"

"Madam," replied Albert, whose vanity was terribly wounded by this sally, "I am at a loss to discover the cause of your merriment."

"You are right, Sir," said Lucie; "such declarations should indeed be no cause for mirth. They ought to be covered with our disdain. Unfortunately, there are women whom like protestations lead astray. I, for instance, know a poor girl who was thus deceived in her affections. She welcomed, with the smile of happiness, mere words of love, like—like those you have just addressed to me; but she soon repented, for he who had sworn to her an eternal attachment, abandoned her a few months after, to shame and misery."

"Why," said Albert, in a tone of raillery, "that certainly is a most affecting story. Yet I don't see your object; in fact, I can't understand you; you are a perfect enigma to me."

"My story would appear, perhaps, less enigmatical, were I to tell you the name of her who was thus abandoned," replied Lucie.

"Ah, yes," drawled Albert; "her name was?—"

"Louisa," replied his cousin.

A shiver ran through Albert's body.

"Well," continued Lucie, "what do you think of it? Is it not odious thus to play with the life and honour of a woman? And must not the man who does so be a wretch, indeed?"

"Take care, Miss Delaborde!" said Albert.

"Take care! why, what's the matter with you, Sir? What is the meaning of your anger? Can this perjured wretch be you?" exclaimed Lucie.

"And who told you this lying story?" asked Albert.

"The victim herself, Sir," replied Lucie; "Louisa, who would now be no more, had I not given her advice and assistance. But you are not listening to me; why should you? You no longer care about the poor girl on whom you have brought both ignominy and wretchedness. I know very well that you have at your disposal golden worlds by which to designate such faults. You call it *killing time*, but I, Sir, call it crime."

"Silence! silence! Lucie," returned Albert, hardly able to contain himself.

"You see, cousin, we should never agree," said Lucie; "so do me a favour to beg my uncle to let me hear no more of this projected marriage."

"I hope you don't suppose," replied Albert, "that I believe this to be your only objection. The fact is, that I've a rival."

"I see no reason, Sir," said Lucie, with great dignity, "to give you any account of my private feelings."

"You hate me, then, Lucie?" inquired Albert.

"It is not you that I hate, Sir, but your vices," replied Miss Delaborde.

While this scene was passing in the private room of the manufacturer, his friend, Baron Barcas, was holding, with Mrs. Delaborde, a conversation of quite a different character, with which the reader will be made acquainted in the next chapter.

IV.

THE PRINCIPLE OF BARON BARCAS

MR. DELABORDE'S first wife had died in giving birth to his son Albert. The manufacturer, however, did not long remain a widower; he soon became enamoured of a young, penniless orphan, of great beauty, and married her. This marriage was brought about by Baron Barcas. Mr. Delaborde, by re-establishing in some measure the Baron's fortune, which this gentleman said had been swallowed up by the Revolution of 1789, had obtained a sure and faithful friend;—such, at least, was his firm conviction, for he consulted the Baron in everything.

Baron Barcas possessed a double face; he could be both frivolous and gay; but, when he threw off the mask, his look was caustic, terrible, or cunning, as he chose; his eye, in which every bad passion sparkled, fascinated and deceived.

Mrs. Delaborde was of small stature, but soft, languid eyes, and a marble complexion gave her the appearance of a beautiful statue. It did not, however, want a very acute eye to see that her body was unanimated by that internal fire which vivifies the look—a soul.

"Ah! Baron," said Mrs. Delaborde, as soon as she perceived her husband's friend, "I was wishing to see you."

"I also, Madam," said the Baron, "was longing to be by your side. Has your health been good during my absence?"

"Not very, Baron," was the reply.

Mrs. Delaborde here looked significantly at Baron Barcas, who, taking the hint, immediately went to see if the door were quite closed.

When certain that no one was outside, "Eleanor," said he, returning quickly to Mrs. Delaborde, "why this change? what has happened?"

"Do you believe in remorse, George?" asked Mrs. Delaborde.

"Certainly, Madam. Remorse is the cancer of weak minds," replied the Baron.

"I deserve this qualification," murmured Mrs. Delaborde, "for when you are no longer here, George, all my tranquillity vanishes. The past rushes to my memory, and becomes my accuser. The recollection of Frederick pursues me continually, and troubles every instant of my life."

"Weak-minded creature!" remarked the Baron, looking at Mrs. Delaborde with the greatest pity.

"Yesterday," continued she, "I was so tormented by these thoughts, that I feared my brain would turn. I left the house alone, in order to avoid meeting with any witnesses of my agitation. I walked I knew not whither. The disorder of my mind carried me on, on, on. I had passed Val-en-Fleurs, but was still without repose. If I raised my eyes towards Heaven, God appeared to me in the lowering clouds, pouring out maledictions on my head. I turned back, but had, however, scarcely entered the meadow, when I heard a step behind me; I looked round, and saw a man following me. I stopped, half dead with fright. He also stopped, and kept his eyes fixed on me. I am sure it was Frederick. In my fear, I took to flight, as if pursued by furies. I dared not even look back, lest my eyes should again alight on that horrid spectre. Fainting and out of breath, I reached home, where I found my husband very uneasy at my absence. I excused myself, by saying that I had been to pay a visit, and Mr. Delaborde is, fortunately, far from suspecting the truth."

"Madam," phlegmatically remarked Baron Barcas, "you will go mad some day."

"Oh! George, how cruel you are!" gasped Mrs. Delaborde.

"Less so than you towards me," added the Baron. "Look, now, what a sad spectacle you offer! A woman, rich, honoured, envied, destroying her own happiness by creating chimerical visions!"

"Oh! George, let me again hear that this was merely the hallucination of my brain," exclaimed Mrs. Delaborde.

"The dead are not, I think, accustomed to return to life," remarked the Baron.

"But is he dead?" eagerly demanded Mrs. Delaborde.

"To convince you, must I fetch his corpse?" asked the Baron. "You know," he added, "as well as I, that Frederick Marvennes, one of the Emperor's warmest partisans, was massacred after the Hundred Days, at Marseilles, with several other officers, at the moment they were about to embark for a foreign land."

"Yes, but this stranger," murmured Mrs. Delaborde, "who has taken up his abode at the Roche-Noire, frightens me excessively. It was, perhaps, he who followed me yesterday. They say that he is rich. He does much charity; yet, why this mystery in which he envelops himself? If he be rich, what makes him live, like a wild beast, in an old ruin? He excites the curiosity of everyone. George, you must find out who he is."

"I hope you will not be silly enough, Eleanor," said the Baron, "to allow yourself to be frightened by an original, who chooses to live like a hermit. It is a way of acquiring celebrity. We are now so accustomed to see people follow the beaten track, that astonishment seizes us when a man dares to lead the life his nature dictates. Society, Madam, is a tyrant that we must either subjugate or serve abjectly."

"Oh, George, no more of your pernicious advice! I'll not listen to it," said Mrs. Delaborde, impatiently: "you promised me happiness, and I have found, in my new position, nothing but bitterness and torment. You deceived me by an odious snare, and snatched from me my child, the only bond that could attach me to honour. Oh! why did I allow myself to be dazzled by the mirage prepared by your infernal hand!"

"These reproaches, Madam," replied George, "are unjust. Since you have forgotten the past, allow me to bring it back to your memory. When I was introduced to you by your old aunt, you were a prey to the most horrible misery—"

"Sir!" exclaimed Mrs. Delaborde, whose pride was deeply wounded. "You proved a treasure to me. I told you that in our society, which is composed of every vice, beauty was a magic sceptre for a woman. You talked to me of honour, and of your duty. In reply, I threw open the window. What was the spectacle we saw? In the middle of the street, we saw a woman, with a child in her arms, shunned and insulted by those of whom she implored charity. A carriage that passed nearly crushed the poor creature. You uttered a cry of horror. Through the carriage windows, was seen a lady, whose beauty and toilet attracted the attention of the crowd. 'Choose,' said I, 'your lot. Be happy and worshipped like this woman, or despised and wretched like that one.' You gave me your answer, Madam, and I carried off your child."

The pale cheeks of Mrs. Delaborde became suffused with scarlet.

"The next day," continued the merciless Baron, "you were arrayed in an elegant dress, of which I made you a present. Your beauty was dazzling. I presented you to Mr. Delaborde, who became enamoured of your charms. A short time afterwards, thanks to the interesting features I had imparted to your orphan youth, you became his wife. The promises I made you, Madam, were realised by this marriage: you possess riches, respect, everything, in fact, that characterises a fortunate existence. So tell me now, how have I deceived you?"

Mrs. Delaborde, vanquished by this satanical logic, and fascinated by the Baron's force of character, quietly repassed under the yoke she had attempted to throw off.

"I have not the right to accuse you," was her sole reply.

A smile of satisfaction played on the Baron's lips.

"It is not just," continued he, "to impute to me the misgivings of your mind, for I have always given you an example of the most unalterable firmness. I have not deviated one jot from the line of conduct I first traced out for myself. My life, however, is the prototype of yours. I have been young, virtuous, humble. I have undergone the pangs of hunger, and felt the cruel humiliations of misfortune. But the day at last came, when, tired of suffering, I boldly raised my head. I looked around and reasoned thus:—'Society is a grand comedy. The skilful and strong choose their parts; the weak and simple accept the characters assigned them. When one is thrown amidst a mass of men who are contending with, and crushing one another, goodness of heart is ridiculous. To grapple with them, one must be made of iron. Life is a steeple-chase,—its goal, riches. Merit and virtue alone obstruct you in your course.' After reasoning thus, I began to practise. A prejudice lent me the aid of its charm; I took a title of nobility. You know how I profited by it. Formerly, my obscure and honest poverty was despised; now I am worshipped as a god. Imitate me, Eleanor; drive from your mind this phantasmagoria of recollections, and forget the past. The past offered you misery and grief; the present has brought you riches, and the future has liberty in reserve for you."

"Liberty! oh, George, how I long to enjoy it!" exclaimed Eleanor.

"You have no complaint, I think, to bring against your husband?" added the Baron. "He accedes, I know, to all your caprices, and his love augments every day."

"And my aversion, George, for him also increases daily," said Mrs. Delaborde. "To be united," she continued, "to a being whom one cannot love is a torture that you know not."

"Patience!" exclaimed the Baron, with a terrible intonation of voice.

"What do you mean?" said Mrs. Delaborde, frightened.

"Oh! fear nothing. I am far from wishing to hasten what natural consequences will bring about," replied the Baron. But, *à propos*, is not your husband engaged at this very moment in informing Lucie of her marriage with his son?"

"I am sure that Lucie will never accept him for her husband," replied Mrs. Delaborde.

"She must," answered the Baron. "Albert, whom I govern as I like, by flattering his tastes, is the very husband to suit us. We must keep a stranger out of the family. Lucie's fortune must not leave us. I am well aware of the repugnance of Mr. Delaborde's niece for this marriage. It is on this account that I persuaded your husband to say it was her mother's wish. Doubtless, this innocent subterfuge will succeed; for Lucie, who adored her mother, will never dare disobey her dying commands. Miss Delaborde does not like us, Madam, and, if we do not bring her to submission, she will become a dangerous enemy."

"You are right, Baron," said Mrs. Delaborde, changing her tone. "And now, come, let us go into the drawing-room."

When Baron Barcas found Albert, he was boiling with rage, and uttering the most atrocious menaces.

"Hallo!" exclaimed his father's friend, "why, what's the matter? This is no good sign."

"Would you believe it?" shrieked Albert; "the little fool has sent me away, after preaching me a sermon. Oh, if I could but find out who is my rival!"

"Ah! now you talk to some purpose," remarked the Baron. "Listen to me, Albert. I once knew a poor devil who was supplanted in his affections by a happy rival. In despair, he thought but of putting an end to his existence, when chance threw him in my way. He made me acquainted with his misfortune. He changed his resolution completely on my recommending him to kill his rival; to enable him to do this, I taught him an infallible thrust, which I place at the disposal of every young man crossed in love. My young friend first insulted his rival—trod on his foot or horsewhipped him—and then sent a sword through his body. A month afterwards, he possessed the woman he loved. In that way, you see, my scientific cut made two persons happy."

"Oh! Baron, you must teach me your famous pass," exclaimed Albert.

"With the greatest pleasure," said the Baron. "This sort of thing is necessary, my dear Albert. Everyone must overthrow the obstacle that rises in his way, and crush his enemy, either by *ruse* or force. *We kill one another*. That is the grand law which governs society. Life is nothing but a combat."

"And I, Baron, will revenge myself on her, by killing the man she loves," added Albert.

"There are other means for achieving our object," continued the Baron. "A severe moralist, however, would, perhaps, find fault with such means. Marriage is sometimes offered to a rebellious young lady as a refuge for her honour. This, though in conformity with the strict rules of morality, must only be employed as a last resource."

"A beautiful idea!" exclaimed Albert. "So, so, my pretty cousin; you will not escape me, after all."

"We must find out, in the first place, Albert, who your rival is," continued the Baron. "Suppose it were——. Oh! no, it cannot be he. Yet, who knows? Love does away with rank."

"What are you saying, Baron?" inquired Albert. "That your rival is, perhaps, Maurice," answered the Baron; "that lout who stopped Lucie's horse, and who, thanks to her, is now employed in the factory. She calls him her preserver! Why, I thought the species was annihilated, and that it existed but in novels. A preserver, indeed! yet that is the name your cousin gives him."

"Oh, no," said Albert, indignantly; "Lucie would never give him the preference over me."

"You are too confident in yourself, Albert," remarked the Baron, who was endeavouring to gall his pupil as much possible. "He is poor, and is, consequently, to be feared. Poverty is incarnate envy. The rich must keep the poor under foot, like a serpent, and crush them as soon as they begin to bite. *They kill one another!*—my grand law again. So keep an eye on this Maurice."

"I will," replied Albert; "but, in the meantime, I should like to learn this famous thrust. I have foils in my room; will you come and show me a little of your dexterity?"

"Willingly. By tomorrow you shall know the secret thrust—One! two! come."

Five minutes afterwards, Albert and Baron Barcas were both busily engaged—the one in teaching, and the other in learning, this famous thrust.

V.

DREAMS OF BLISS

PARTLY by superiority of mind, and partly by the influence obtained through a crest of nobility, was the manufacturer held in subjection by Baron Barcas, who, at the same time, governed Mrs. Delaborde by terror, and Albert by vice.

Baron Barcas was haughty or supple, according to the persons with whom he had to deal. Everyone feared and conciliated him, for he possessed two terrible weapons with which to overthrow his enemies—sarcasm, and a sword; and both were equally destructive. More, than one antagonist had succumbed beneath the edge of his satire; more than one duellist had been laid helpless at his feet. Among his many acts of prowess, he had struck out of the list of the living a certain lawyer, who had inspired Mrs. Delaborde with too tender feelings. This circumstance had gained him the friendship of the manufacturer in particular, and the approbation of husbands in general. The Baron was extremely opposed to the marriage of Albert with any other woman but his cousin Lucie. He distinctly saw that the introduction of a stranger into the family would prove most pernicious to his projects; but he had nothing to fear from Lucie, when once married, for her uncle paid no attention to anything she said. Poor Lucie! she would have been much happier anywhere else but with the family of the manufacturer. Hated by Mrs. Delaborde and the Baron, and watched over by the jealous eye of her cousin, she found her uncle's house had become her prison, the very atmosphere of which oppressed her heart and mind. Her words were maliciously interpreted; her actions calumniated. She discovered, in the hypocritical advice given to her, the coldness of hatred, and her enemies wished to impress on her that her marriage with Albert was the sole condition of reconciliation. They hoped, by this sullen persecution, to force her inclination. How they were deceived! Like all persons of firm resolution, Lucie would have sooner died than bend to despotism. At the same time, she was animated by a sentiment which will ever prove stronger than hatred. She loved a pale and melancholy young man, who often passed before her window, exchanging a glance with her. What volumes did their looks contain! At the age when love bursts forth, the heart, however compressed, will, by destroying all opposing dykes, ever find an issue for its streams of hope.

Lucie, however, at last gave way to sadness. The object of her love had disappeared. It was in vain that she opened her window, in vain that she looked around; he was never near. Oh! how sad she felt! From that time her life changed. The persecutions to which she was subject appeared more poignant.

One evening, after an altercation with her cousin, Lucie stole from her uncle's house. It had been very hot all day; the sun was then sinking into a bed of golden clouds; the air resounded with a thousand sounds—melancholy adieus, which the evening seemed to address to the fleeting day. She was no longer constrained, no longer obliged to watch her every action; she was free, and gave herself up to a sweet reverie. The exuberance of nature appeared to increase her strength; and the breeze, playing gently with her long silky tresses, imparted a beautiful colour to her cheeks. She was walking on rapidly, when she met, at the end of a meadow, near a hedge, a young man, who tried to avoid her.

"Maurice!" she exclaimed.

"Miss Delaborde!" coldly replied the person addressed; and he endeavoured to go on.

"Why do you avoid me, Maurice?" asked Lucie.

"Because respect, Madam, tells me to do so," he replied. "You, I know, are obliged to maintain your rank, and to keep persons of my station at a distance."

"Have you, then, forgotten," said Lucie, "how much I owe you? Had it not been for you, I should not, at this moment, be alive."

"I do not merit so much gratitude for an action a thousand others would have been as happy to do in my place," replied Maurice. "I followed the impulse of my heart, that was all. I must beg you, Miss Delaborde, to allow me to leave you. I should be much afflicted if, in your present situation, when you are on the eve of contracting a union with your cousin, we were to be seen together by Mr. Albert, who treats me with such haughty disdain."

Lucie was now made acquainted with the cause of Maurice's disappearance and change of manner.

"No one has the right to treat you with disdain, Maurice," said she, "and my cousin less than anyone else. Has not your ability placed you over all my uncle's workmen? But let us talk of my marriage; you cannot dislike to speak of it."

"On the contrary," replied Maurice, with an effort to master his emotion, "everything concerning your happiness will be willingly listened to by me."

Whether she were influenced by that apparently natural inclination of women to torment to beings who are dear to them, or love, Miss Delaborde added, in a slightly ironical tone, "And will you come to my wedding, Maurice? I hope, at least, that you will not carry your respect so far as to refuse me a favour I so much desire."

"Madam," stammered out Maurice, "such a thing would be impossible. I could not—"

"Ah! I see," said Miss Delaborde, "I am still too proud. Must I, then, own that it is my most ardent wish to see you at the celebration of my marriage."

In the presence of such cruel obstinacy, the studied calm of Maurice forsook him entirely. The passion, which was but ill-pent-up in his heart, burst forth.

"Listen to me, Lucie," said he, with a voice trembling with emotion. "There was once a man—he must have then been mad—who, though poor and obscure, dared to cast his eyes on you, who are endowed with both beauty and riches. He loved you with all the power of a burning soul. You seem surprised! you have the right to be so. Between the different classes of society there are lines of demarcation, plainly drawn: I am aware of this, and so was he. But the heart knows no barriers, no distinctions; its impulse drives it towards the highest as well as towards the humblest creature. This poor fool met, however, with terrible punishment, merely for having forgotten, for an instant, that fortune accords every joy, and every kind of happiness, while poverty cancels even the right to love. He was nearly bereft of his senses, on hearing of your marriage with Mr. Albert. Reason, however, came to his assistance. He had the courage to stifle his passion. His imagination conjured up a dream, in which the realization of his happiness was promised in heaven. But now, when this fire, which burnt within his breast, is scarcely extinguished; when his thoughts of happiness are but half vanished, you come and ask him to be present at the triumph of his rival—the sight would kill him."

To this burst of vehemence Lucie gently replied, "Take care, Maurice; grief often makes us unjust. In these privileged classes, against which you are so bitter, are still found persons with minds elevated enough to prefer merit and obscure birth to the artificial and painted life so often forced upon them. But like Laocoon, stifled in the folds of the serpents of Tenedos, it is often in vain for them to struggle with the prejudices that surround them."

Maurice seemed struck with a sudden light.

"Lucie," he exclaimed, with exultation, "can I believe such happiness? and will you forget the reproaches of a madman, whom the thunder of heaven ought to have struck down for accusing so courageous and virtuous a being as yourself?"

"I thought, Maurice, that there was no love without faith," said Miss Delaborde.

"Pardon me, Lucie," replied Maurice, "but I suffered so much at the thought of losing you forever. They talk all over the town of nothing but your marriage with Mr. Albert. Tell me, am I to believe this report?"

"That report is spread by Baron Barcas and my amiable cousin," replied Lucie. "They hope, by their falsehoods, to weaken my resistance; but my firmness will never yield to their base manœvres. I now swear to you, Maurice, that if ever I wed Albert Delaborde, he will take his bride home a corpse."

"Oh! what misery it is," exclaimed Maurice, "to see you surrounded by enemies, and not to be able to come to your assistanc! To be a man, whom, if his love for you were known, they would drive like a menial from the house! My soul is indignant at the thought that you must blush for me. I would give my life's blood to wipe away the unjust disdain visited on my station. If I had not seen you, Lucie, I should have felt content with an humble lot; but now I begin to dream of future glory! To be worthy of you, I would strain every nerve. Perhaps I shall, some day, be able, by incessant toil, to attain the position that I long for. If I ever do, oh! what happiness will be mine!"

"That you may overcome all obstacles, Maurice, shall be my constant prayer," said Lucie.

"Oh, madness!" exclaimed the young man, in a voice which made Lucie tremble; "such happiness will never be mine. There, leave me, Lucie; forget me altogether; my shame shall never fall on you."

"What! have you still another secret?" said Lucie, softly.

"Oh, yes, a terrible one. I am without a name—without a family!" exclaimed Maurice, convulsively.

"Are you not the son of Jérôme Ballue, and Juliette's brother?" asked Lucie.

"No, Lucie," replied Maurice; "my mother was seduced, and then abandoned. Despised by everyone, without a place in which to shelter her head, she died on the high road leading to Saint George, where he, whom I call my father, found me. Generous and compassionate, the good old man brought me up as his son, but society does not for all that the less proscribe me. You see, Lucie, the magic power even of an angel is not enough to turn aside the fatality that pursues me."

"Hope still, Maurice," said Lucie, in a voice so soft and penetrating that it dispelled his despondency. Not able to master his feelings, he fell at her feet, and seizing her hand covered it with kisses.

"Whatever may happen now," exclaimed Maurice, rising, "I shall be happy with my life."

At this instant, a diabolical laugh, as if repeated from echo to echo, broke the silence of the night. The two lovers remained motionless, struck with terror.

"Great Heaven! can anyone have been listening?" whispered Lucie.

Maurice was over the hedge in a moment. Nobody was, however, to be seen there.

"'This fancy, perhaps," said Maurice, returning, and endeavouring to calm Lucie's fears; "or perhaps," continued he, half joking, half serious, "'twas Satan, got behind the hedge to laugh at me."

Maurice was right. Baron Barcas had followed Lucie, and, hidden behind the hedge, had listened attentively to their conversation.

The lovers, frightened by the Baron's satanical laugh, immediately separated, each taking a different direction.

VI.

THE WORKMEN

BARON BARCAS was fully aware that constant intercourse augments the passion of lovers, but that time and absence are sure to diminish it. When unfed, the fire dies. This would be the case, he said, with Lucie's romantic love. The only means of assuring her marriage with her cousin was to hinder her from seeing Maurice. The thing necessary to bring about was a disagreement between Mr. Delaborde and his foreman: this was no easy task. The manufacturer liked Maurice exceedingly, for in him he possessed a foreman who was of immense service in the direction of the manufactory. Nothing, however, appeared impossible to Baron Barcas. His fertile imagination soon furnished him with a means of realising his project. He told the manufacturer that the price he gave for labour was higher than that given in other places, and that he ought to lower it. Mr. Delaborde, who willingly listened to all the Baron said, believed this, and immediately altered his rate of payment. The workmen, refusing to accept their reduced wages, struck directly. The astute Baron had foreseen this. Their strike was approved of by Maurice, who promised to get the old rate of payment reestablished. For this purpose, he demanded an interview with Mr. Delaborde.

"Well," said the manufacturer, "what is the meaning of this? The workmen have struck, I hear. What is their object in so doing? Do they think to hurt me? Why, before a week, I could obtain elsewhere ten times the number of hands."

"I hope, Sir," replied Maurice, "that you will not have recourse to such an expedient. I am come to second the demands of the men. They had been paid for years according to the old tariff, and I am sure, Sir, that you will not think it just to change it."

"Oh, you must speak to the Baron," replied Mr. Delaborde, who had nothing to answer.

"I prefer speaking to you, Sir," said Maurice, "because I never found you averse, like Baron Barcas, to listen to the truth. You would not like to make beggars of your workmen, most of whom have been with you above ten years. While you have grown rich, Sir, they have still remained poor; and you ought, Sir, to remember past services by maintaining the old rate of payment."

This reasoning did not at all suit Mr. Delaborde, who was about to reply sharply, when a furious noise in the yard called his attention thither.

"What is this noise?" said he to Maurice.

The young man opened the window, and showed Mr. Delaborde his two hundred workmen, who, with their wives and families, were assembled before the house.

"Look, Sir," said Maurice; "they are there, waiting to hear their fate. Oh! you will not be the cause of an impious war between the rich and poor. Recollect, they are struggling for their daily bread, the very existence of their families. It is a happy thing to be rich. You have but to pronounce a word, and all those people, whom you see, at present so sad, before you, will proclaim you their benefactor, and teach their children to bless your name."

Mr. Delaborde would have, no doubt, yielded to the vehement pleading of his foreman, had not the arrival of the Baron and Albert changed his position.

The new comers guessed in an instant how things stood. Maurice saw his cause was lost.

"Do you know what has taken place?" said Baron Barcas to the manufacturer, with great gravity. "All your men have turned out, and are howling like so many wild beasts. I just now heard, as I was passing, the most atrocious menaces uttered against yourself."

"I thought the scoundrels," chimed in Albert, "would have torn us to pieces. Had it not been for the Baron's presence of mind, I should have been killed."

An uproar, more menacing and terrible than the first, now arose to justify the assertions of Albert and his friend. Mr. Delaborde became deadly pale; he shivered in all his limbs.

"Tranquillize yourself," said the Baron, who perceived the manufacturer's fear; "I have informed the police. Orders have already been given for dispersing these horrid creatures. But, Sir, a fitting punishment must befal the instigator of this revolt. You must punish him who, profiting by his influence over your men, advised them to quit their work, by saying: 'Menace, and you will be listened to.'"

"Punish! oh, yes; that I will. But do you know who it is? Can you point out to me?" said the manufacturer, simulating rage, in order to hide his fear.

"He is now before you," said the Baron, pointing at Maurice.

"Maurice!" exclaimed Mr. Delaborde, astonished.

"I entirely deny what the Baron imputes to me," said Maurice. "It was I, on the contrary, who recommended the workmen to be moderate in their demands."

"It's a lie," impudently exclaimed the Baron. "Do those persons, now, who are at present howling like wild beasts, seem disposed to be moderate?"

The noise increased at this instant. "Come, Mr. Maurice," continued the Baron, in an exulting tone, "since you are the hero of this revolt, show yourself at the window, and appease, these madmen."

"I never yet practised deception anywhere," bluntly replied Maurice, "and were I to appear now at the window, they would fancy that their demands have been complied with."

"Maurice," said Mr. Delaborde, pale from fright, "leave my house directly."

The Baron's face was lighted up with a diabolical look of satisfaction.

"I am grieved, Sir, to see you yield to the malignant suggestions of Baron Barcas," said Maurice, with great firmness. "For myself, I leave your house, Sir, with the conviction of having done my duty."

"What! are you going to leave us Maurice?" exclaimed Lucie, who had just entered.

"It is your uncle's order," replied Maurice.

"Oh, it cannot be," said Miss Delaborde. "Uncle, you have not given such an order, have you? Maurice is not guilty. Of what do you accuse him? He cannot leave. You will not allow him, will you?"

"What! Lucie," remarked Albert, scornfully, "can you degrade yourself, by defending this low fellow?"

At this insult, Maurice was about to spring on Albert. A look from Lucie held him back.

"Low! Sir. I scarcely understand you," replied Lucie. "Maurice once saved my life at the peril of his own; a thing that you had not the courage to attempt on a like occasion." Albert bit his lips, and turned towards his friend.

"Uncle," continued Lucie, "it is not your intention to drive Maurice from your house, is it?"

"I never retract what I have once said. Maurice *must* leave," replied Mr. Delaborde.

"Well!" replied Lucie, "since he must go, I will go too; for I love him!"

The manufacturer was stupified by this avowal.

The Baron, sufficiently well informed, had been waiting for this moment.

"So, Lucie, this is the cause of all your disobedience!" said Mr. Delaborde.

"Listen to me for an instant, uncle," replied his niece. "You promised my mother, on her deathbed, to assure my happiness. The only way to do so is to allow me to marry Maurice. With him alone can I be happy. You would reduce me to despair, by forcing me to wed another. Maurice has, I know, no fortune, but I have enough for both of us."

"You must be mad, Lucie!" exclaimed the manufacturer.

The Baron burst into a loud malignant laugh. Maurice and Lucie shuddered: they had already heard that sardonic yell.

"In good truth," remarked he, in a tone of profound surprise, "I can scarcely believe my ears. What! Mr. Maurice has pretensions to the hand of the rich heiress of Maria Storeni! It must be a joke. Has he forgotten that he is the son of a miserable woman, an abandoned creature? Must I tell him that his birth even was a crime, and that he was found on the road leading to Saint-George, near his mother's corpse, and brought up, out of charity, by Jérôme Ballue, a poor schoolmaster? These details must certainly be unknown to Miss Delaborde, for I cannot suppose that she would be willingly dishonour her family. Tell me, Mr. Maurice, am I a good historian?"

Maurice, his eyes starting from their sockets, rushed towards the Baron.

"Silence!" cried he; "another word, and I fell you to the ground. Not content with ruining me, your slanderous tongue must calumniate my mother, a fallen martyr. Oh! you must, indeed, be a coward, thus to attack the memory of a woman. Baron Barcas, you are a lying, cowardly scoundrel."

The Baron's face assumed a terrible expression, but, in order to throw no obstacle in his own way, he hid his resentment under a smile of contempt.

"Adieu, Miss Lucie!" said Maurice, whose sobs nearly choked him. "Forget Maurice, who will forget you but with death. Had I been born rich and happy, like Mr. Albert, or noble, like his friend, I should have been permitted to remain with you, but Heaven has not willed it thus. Adieu! The son of Magdalene Simon must be resigned. His mother set him the example."

Mr. Delaborde's head swan.

"My son!" murmured he, falling into a chair, as Maurice left the room.

Lucie, in tears, withdrew into her chamber to weep at liberty.

The attention of the Baron was fixed on the manufacturer, whose emotion caused him to reflect.

"Can I have killed two birds with one stone?" said he. "I did not think I was so skilful;" and he left the room with Albert.

When alone, Mr. Delaborde breathed more freely. A thousand confused ideas filled his head.

"Maurice!" said he, wiping away large drops of perspiration which ran down his forehead. "Maurice! found on the road leading to Saint-George, near the corpse of his mother! Oh, Heaven! That dying woman, for whom I had so little pity on the night of the ninth of January, was Magdalen: that cry of despair, which still rings in my ears, was hers. Oh! wretched man! 'Tis I who have killed her! I who have driven Maurice from my house!"

After this tribute to his conscience, the manufacturer fell into his usual state. Reflection, or rather calculation, made him consider this event in another light. The sensitive man disappeared, and was succeeded with the calculating, selfish man of business, whose heart is a receipt stamp, and whose head is a multiplication table. "What a thing for me," said he, "if it had been discovered that Maurice is my son! What reproaches I should have had to endure! A separation would have ensued. Besides, his presence would have recalled to my mind the recollection of Magdalen. Considering all things, I have got out of it pretty well."

The manufacturer approved of this last operation of his by a most self-applauding smile.

VII.

FREDERICK MARVENNES

ELEANOR BARETTE, suddenly transported from an attic into a sumptuous mansion, and changing the privations of poverty for the enjoyment of wealth, was, for a time, dazzled by her new position. She soon found herself, however, in the iron grasp of Baron Barcas. She suffered so much the more from this subjection, because her character was naturally imbued with the most invincible pride. This passion had been the cause of all her faults. To satisfy it, she had neglected the duties of the mother, and vanquished the aversions of the woman.

On escaping from poverty, Eleanor had not, however, met with happiness. Had she lived at Paris, in the midst of noise and pleasure, she would have, perhaps, forgotten the past, but the silence of her villa at Tours, caused her the most terrible qualms of conscience. The recollection of Frederick

Marvennes gnawed, like a serpent, incessantly into her heart.

Thanks to the agitation that Maurice's dismissal had caused, no one thought of Mrs. Delaborde, who, a prey to the most abject despondency, had retired to her own room. She was trying every means to drive away the dark presentiments of evil from her mind, when the servant announced a visitor. Eleanor immediately found hers in the presence of a man, who, motionless as a statue, turned on her the light of his eyes, which shone like balls of fire. Terrified, Eleanor drew back, and fell, nearly senseless, on the sofa.

Any other but she would have been unable to recognise Frederick Marvennes. Sixteen years had wrought great changes in him. The man who stood before her was no longer the handsome officer of former times. Grief was now deeply depicted on those features where once the haughty look and smile of confidence shone so conspicuously. Though he still retained his martial figure, sorrow had furrowed his brow, and Eleanor herself seemed to doubt; for, she said, in the firmest tones she could command:—

"Who are you, Sir, and what do you want?"

"You ask me, Madam, two very brief questions, which it will take a long time to answer," replied Frederick. "Who am I? The answer is a long one. Are you disposed to listen to it?"

"Yes, Sir," replied Mrs. Delaborde, hardly conscious of what she said.

"You must recollect, Madam," began Frederick, "the terror which oppressed France, after the Hundred Days. The brave men who had valiantly fought for their county, at Waterloo, were forced to fly before bands of assassins. The Royalists tracked them like wild beasts, and massacred them without pity. Among other officers, Frederick Marvennes was the first to desert the cause of Louis XVIII. for that of Napoleon. He was, in consequence, condemned to death. The possession of two beings—a woman, whom he ardently loved, and a child—made him cling most tenaciously to life. After having escaped the massacre at Marseilles, and a thousand other dangers, he reached a foreign land in safety. But he did not much regret leaving France, then in the hands of cowardly assassins, for Eleanor, his affianced, had sworn to protect the child of their love. But what is the matter, Madam? you appear affected."

"Your story, Sir, has touched me," wildly exclaimed Mrs. Delaborde.

"As soon as Frederick Marvennes had arrived safely in Switzerland, he wrote to Eleanor, to inform her of the name had had taken, and to beg her to let him hear from her. His letter received no answer. Again and again he wrote, but only again to experience the same bitter disappointment. A prey to the greatest uneasiness, and fearing that something had happened to the mother of his child, he braved all dangers, and returned to France. He knocked at the attic-door of his affianced. A strange face opened it. He inquired for Eleanor Barette, and was informed that she had left her home one morning, richly dressed, in the company of a gentleman. Can you picture what were the feelings of Frederick, on learning that she, who, at his departure, had sworn a thousand oaths of love and fidelity, had abandoned herself to another? His heart was broken, Madam. But you are trembling."

Eleanor made no reply; the palpitations of her heart, however, but too plainly told the emotion she was labouring under.

"Mad with grief, Frederick no longer attempted to hide himself. He was arrested, and thrown into prison. He remained there ten years, tortured by anxiety and doubt; for he was utterly ignorant of the fate of his child. Restored at last to freedom, in 1825, the unhappy man arrived in time to witness the last moments of an old uncle, who left him a large fortune. But what were riches now to him? He would have given all his wealth for one kiss from the daughter, whose fate he had wept over for ten years, within the walls of his prison. But Frederick still fancied that his daughter lived. Encouraged by a gleam of hope, he began to seek for Eleanor, found her, and appeared one day before her. But can you imagine how she received him, Madam? Oh, you will never believe such conduct! More shameless than a courtesan, she asked him who he was, and what he wanted?"

Frederick advanced towards Mrs. Delaborde, and, seizing her hands, apostrophized her with these terrible words: "What crime have you, then, committed, to tremble thus?"

"Pity!" exclaimed Eleanor, terrified by the looks of her accuser.

"Providence had entrusted to your care an innocent creature. What have you done with it?" cried Frederick.

"Pity, Frederick! pity! I have not forgotten you!" gasped Eleanor.

"Oh, do not imagine, Madam," continued Frederick, "that I have sought you, for five years, merely to address to you the reproaches of a deceived lover. No; I come to demand my daughter. She still lives, does she not? Tell me where she is, and you shall be no further troubled. Say, where is my daughter?"

"I know not," answered Mrs. Delaborde, in so low a tone that Frederick scarcely heard her.

"Oh, infamy! Have you, then, committed an infanticide?" exclaimed he.

"Does a mother kill her child?" asked Eleanor. "Listen to me, Frederick, and I will tell you the whole truth. At Paris, I was without work, and was verging on the last stage of want. An infernal tempter came and offered me the means of alleviating my misery. He fascinated me by the perspective of a brilliant marriage. In order, however, to contract this marriage, it was necessary to deceive Mr. Delaborde, and I was obliged to give up my child. I had lost all hope of seeing you again, as I thought you had been massacred at Marseilles; I therefore agreed to everything. The man, however, to whom I confided my child, and who promised to have it brought up secretly, betrayed me. He placed it, one night, on the steps of Saint Roch's, and then waited behind a pillar, until he saw a man, attracted by the cries of the child, approach, and carry it away. This, Frederick, is the truth. Do not prove too severe a judge; I have already suffered too much."

"And you," exclaimed Frederick, "you can indulge, without remorse, in all the luxuries of wealth, while your daughter is, perhaps, begging her bread from door to door?"

"Oh, silence! Frederick, pity! Silence!" breathed Eleanor; "if they were to hear you, I should be lost! Speak lower! speak lower!"

"Ah! you are afraid of appearing in your real character. You are, I know, admired and respected;

you are Queen of Tours, the centre of attraction, and the leader of the fashion. But if you were shown in your true light, you would immediately become an object of contempt. I can well understand how your pride would suffer. The atonement would be a cruel one, yet you shall make it," said Frederick, in a voice of thunder.

"Oh, no, Frederick!" cried Eleanor, writhing in despair, "you cannot mean it. You cannot have the heart thus to dishonour me."

"So you thought," continued Frederick, "that, to efface your crimes, nothing more was necessary than to throw over them the golden cloak of riches! But I will tear it from your shoulders, and expose to the view of all the hideous form it hides. Do you hear me?"

"Oh! Frederick, do not drive me mad," said Eleanor, imploringly; "do not ruin me forever. Take pity on me."

"Did you take pity on your daughter? Kneel, woman without honour; mother without feeling, kneel!"

Mrs. Delaborde fell at Frederick's feet. Steps were heard approaching. Eleanor tried to rise, but all the power to do so had left her, and she fell fainting on the ground.

Mr. Delaborde and the Baron entered. The manufacturer was advancing in a menacing attitude towards Mr. Marvennes, when the latter stopped him, with a gesture full of dignity.

"I possessed a right over this woman, Sir, before you," said Frederick; "prior to becoming your wife, she was already a mother, and my affianced."

"Give me proof of this, Sir," said Mr. Delaborde; "give me proof of what you say, or—"

Frederick let fall at the manufacturer's feet a packet of letters. The Baron's rage equalled the stupefaction of his friend. Frederick Marvennes moved slowly towards the door, turned round two or three times, to look at the personages of this scene, and then left the room.

"Oh! I'll revenge myself," murmured Mrs. Delaborde, as Frederick went out.

The astonished husband picked up the packet of letters, and begged the Baron to go with him to his private room. As soon as they had entered, Mr. Delaborde, no longer able to contain his fury, said to the Baron: "So, Sir, you have acted like an impostor towards me!"

"Come, let us be more polite," replied the Baron, "we can discuss this matter less angrily."

"You are sarcastic, as usual, Sir," said Mr. Delaborde; "but your time is ill-chosen. I will no longer be your dupe, do you hear? I will not remain with the woman who has deceived me, but obtain a separation. It will be a scandalous exposure, but I shall not be the person who will have cause the blush."

"You shall do nothing of the sort, my dear Sir," said the Baron.

"And why not?" asked Mr. Delaborde.

"Because if you did," answered his friend, "Maurice should know tomorrow that you are his father."

VIII.

FRIENDS

MRS. DELABORDE underwent the chastisement with which Frederick had threatened her. A local paper published the history of her youth. Although she was not named in the account, everyone recognised her. She witnessed the realization of Frederick's prediction. She was despised by all, and especially by those women who had to hide faults similar to her own. In order to escape the humiliations she endured—humiliations that were doubly felt in a place of which she had been, as it were, the queen—Eleanor induced her husband to give up his manufactory, and leave Tours. Mr. Delaborde readily yielded to her solicitations; they, therefore, removed to Paris, where she could easily bury her shame, and where she could, at least, be sheltered from the gaze of those who, after the exposure, watched her every movement.

On leaving prison, the only object for which the heart of Frederick Marvennes beat, was his daughter. We have seen how cruel was the blow he received in his paternal love.

Tired, at length, of being made the playtime of fate, Frederick abandoned himself to a life of revelry, in the hope of giving the finishing stroke to the work which Eleanor had so well begun. This had continued for six months, which appeared six centuries to Frederick, when, at the end of January, he gave a masked ball, to celebrate the Carnival. Frederick was not in a very gay mood that evening; *ennui* pervaded his whole system; yet this was the most brilliant ball he had ever given. In order, therefore, not to throw a damp over the gaiety of his guests, he retired into the reception-room, where his thoughts immediately wandered towards his daughter.

He had hardly seated himself, however, when he heard the approach of a swarm of friends.

"Oh, could I but avoid them!" he murmured.

Four persons entered the room; a banker, a poet, a conservative member, and a melodramatic author.

"It's prodigious! not to be believed," vociferated Edmund St. Phar, the poet; "he *is* here. Stop up all the holes, so that he can't creep out. Mr. Boulard, get before the door."

"Here I am," replied the member, "he has no chance to escape."

"What a wonderful man!" remarked the banker. "He is in deep reflection, while all the rest are dancing!"

"My dear friend, I was very uneasy about you," said Theodor, the melodramatic author, who entitled himself the Pylades of Mr. Marvennes.

Frederick listened to these protestations of friendship, without moving a muscle.

"Gentlemen," said St. Phar, in a lugubrious voice, "I invite you to the internment of Mr. Frederick Marvennes; so a *de profundis,* if you please."

At this, the three others laughed aloud.

"If we had received such an invitation by letter," continued the poet, "finding a corpse would not have surprised us; but I cannot imagine how anyone has the courage to resist the poetry of a masked ball!"

"Or the charms of women," said the conservative member.

"Or this divine music," said the melodramatic author.

"Or the display of dress, the sparkling of diamonds and jewels," added the banker.

"He has no poetry in him," continued the poet.

"He belongs to neither sex," added the lawmaker.

"He is made of stone," remarked Theodore, "and yet the rocks moved at the divine sounds of Orpheus's lyre."

"And I," screamed the banker, "maintain that he is blind."

"Gentlemen," mysteriously remarked Theodore, "there must be in our friend's past life some sombre event, the colour of which darkens his present moments."

"Why, really," remarked St. Phar, "I think I discover in his face the ferocious expression of a brigand tormented by remorse."

"What an astonishing man!" cried the banker.

"After all," exclaimed St. Phar, "we are his friends, and he has not the right to hide his thoughts from us. My dear Marvennes, in the name of our friendship, we implore you to open your soul to us."

"My spirits are low," replied Frederick, gasping. "Find me an efficacious remedy for melancholy, and I will esteem you my best friends. In what does happiness consist?"

"In good living," said the conservative member.

"In poetry," replied the poet.

"In riches," said the banker.

"In music," chimed in the melodramatic author.

"According to you," remarked Frederick, "happiness is everywhere."

At this moment, the joyous hubbub of the ball-room ceased, as if by enchantment, and a dead silence followed. This again was succeeded by a confused noise of murmurs, of whispers, and of exclamations of surprise. The joy of the guests had evidently been troubled by some serious event. The member, poet, and banker went to see what this was owing to. Theodore profited by this opportunity to overwhelm Frederick with protestations of friendship. The three others soon returned. They were uneasy and agitated.

"My dear Marvennes," said St. Phar, "I must leave you to see my mother home."

"Why have they stopped dancing?" asked Frederick.

The three friends looked at each other with embarrassment.

"You must excuse me, too, Mr. Marvennes," said the banker; "my wife is putting on her shawl."

Mr. Boulard made a like excuse, and, before leaving the room, whispered a word to Theodore. The melodramatic author opened his eyes with surprise.

"Wait for me an instant, gentlemen," he shouted, "I shall go with you, for company. My dear friend," said he, turning to Frederick, "I am very sorry to leave you alone, but I also have somebody waiting for me. You will excuse me, I know; goodbye." And

Frederick's *soi-disant* friend walked away as fast as his legs would carry him.

"What can be the meaning of all this?" said Frederick, placing himself so as to obtain a full view of his apartments.

His astonishment was great indeed, when he saw his guests hurriedly hastening towards the hall door, which was too narrow for the impatient crowd.

"This is very strange!" said Frederick. "Is my house on fire? Or has any accident happened? Perhaps this letter, that I received before the ball commenced, and that I have not opened, will inform me. Let me see."

Frederick drew a letter from his pocket-book. "My banker has fled—gone abroad—leaving a deficit of a million!" exclaimed he, after reading the letter. "I am ruined!" He crushed the letter in his hand, and then threw it away, without betraying the least emotion. "It seems," added he, while looking with pity and contempt at the crowd rushing through the hall, "that a ruined man is a very dangerous person. Fools! I offered them a banquet, to which they came, bowing to the ground. Now, when they have satiated themselves, they quit my table, and avoid me. What a vile and lying world this is! The dog to which we throw a bone is less ungrateful. Really, my indignation is thrown away;

such a sight was worth the whole of my fortune. Now, I will go and see whether the same things are to be witnessed in the sombre abode of Pluto. My pistols are ready; yet I did not expect to have to use them so soon. But then I reckoned without my banker." After this soliloquy, Frederick went into his study. He soon returned, carrying in his hand a case, which he placed on a chair. On turning round, he found himself in the presence of a woman, in a rose-coloured domino, whose eyes flashed fire through the holes of her mask. "Have I still a friend?" exclaimed Frederick.

"No, Mr. Marvennes," replied the person addressed, taking off her mask, "you see in me an enemy, come to satisfy her vengeance."

"Eleanor!" exclaimed the ruined man, thunderstruck.

IX.

ONE FOOT IN THE GRAVE

ELEANOR triumphed; a savage joy pervaded her features, and she seemed, by her haughty attitude, to set Frederick at defiance.

"You little thought to see me again!" said she, in a tone of irony. "You, no doubt, imagined you had crushed me by your cowardly denunciations. My thirst for revenge has continued to rise with the weight of my shame, which has increased every time I have thought of that dreadful day. To be able to revenge myself has been my hope and consolation night and day; I followed you to Paris, surrounded you with spies, and thus learnt all you did: I heard that you had become a man of fashion; that you were rich and happy. How I longed to hurl you from your pedestal! To accomplish that object, I strained every nerve; no sacrifice was spared to bring about your ruin, and, when my object was attained, I came here, and stigmatized you, in the midst of all present, with these three words:—'He is ruined!' To those who would not believe, I showed irrefutable proofs; my voice threw dismay among your guests; they immediately deserted your ball, and every friend left you. These rooms, which, but a few moments ago, were filled with joyful sounds, are now as sad and silent as the grave; I alone remain. Oh! you must have been mad, after having so publicly outraged a woman, to abandon yourself quietly to a life of pleasure, without even thinking it necessary to take means for warding off impending danger. Listen, Frederick, and know what misery is; it is hourly-increasing torment—suffering of body and soul combined; it is impotent despair, daily decline, craving of the stomach. Shame and disease, those stigmas placed by society on the features of her fated children, belong to misery, and of misery shall your life henceforth be made up. Ignominy shall be yours, and you yourself accursed!"

While Eleanor was pouring out these words of fury, Frederick drew a pistol from his pocket; she had not perceived this, for the pleasure of revenge completely blinded her. When she had done speaking, Frederick stepped before her, and, holding the pistol to her head, said:—

"It appears to me, Madam, that you wish to be sarcastic."

Eleanor's terror was so great that she nearly fell; she tried to speak, but the words expired on her pale and trembling lips.

"Misery, I see," continued Frederick, "by the sketch you have drawn of it, is indeed a dreadful companion; I have, therefore, no wish to try it. It is preferable, I think, to die of a pistol shot; yet this mode of death is not over-agreeable; is it, Madam?"

Eleanor trembled in every limb; the murderous weapon, still threatening her, made her suffer the tortures of a thousand deaths.

"Oh, Frederick," said she, joining her hands, "I beseech you, take away that dreadful pistol; it will drive me mad."

"You had not sufficiently reflected, Madam," replied Frederick, "before commencing to play with a ruined man; it is a great risk to menace a man who has nothing but misery in perspective, that is, *hourly-increasing torment, suffering of body and soul combined.*

"Oh! you cannot mean to assassinate me, Frederick. You would not wish to mount the scaffold!" ejaculated Eleanor.

"You, yourself, Eleanor," replied Frederick, "would undergo that infamous punishment, if human justice could overtake those wretched women who, like you, make a traffic of the heart's pulsations, tread under foot the most sacred duties, and turn their beauty into a snare by which to sacrifice the honour of whole families. But, as you escape the justice of man, I, in the name of the justice of Heaven, will, myself, undertake your punishment!"

This was said in so solemn a tone, that Eleanor imagined she heard the judgment of an avenging Heaven.

"Oh! I cannot die thus!" cried she, in the greatest agony. "Someone will come to my assistance."

"No one will come to your assistance, for you have taken care to frighten everyone away. *Your voice has thrown dismay among my guests. They have deserted my ball: every friend has left me.* You see, you have yourself dug your grave."

"Oh! forgive me, Frederick. I repent! I repent!" shrieked Eleanor.

"It is too late," replied Frederick. "Come, make your peace with Heaven; or rather with Satan, for you must have a long account to settle with the latter!"

"Oh! you cannot be abandoned enough to turn assassin!" gasped Eleanor.

"Whenever I meet a serpent I crush it without mercy," replied Frederick.

"Do not be inexorable!" exclaimed Eleanor, bathed in tears, and falling at his feet. "Let me live, and I swear to expiate my faults. My fortune—

everything I have, shall be yours. But do not kill me, do not kill me!"

"Then you dread death, Eleanor!" said Frederick.

"Oh! yes; to die is frightful!" replied Eleanor.

"You are right," added Frederick, solemnly. "When we are afraid to appear before Heaven—when we have despised every duty of life, and prostituted our souls to worldly things, it must indeed be a frightful thing to die."

"Do not curse me! I am afraid—afraid!" murmured Mrs. Delaborde.

"Eleanor, you are a coward. Rise. I would not degrade myself by taking the life of so mean a thing! Go back to the position you hold in the world, of which you are such a worthy representative. Go!"

Frederick made way for her to pass; and Mrs. Delaborde, hardly recovered from her terror, hastened from the room.

"And now," said Frederick, as soon as she was gone, "why should I hesitate? What is there for me to do here? I lead a miserable and useless existence; disgust and lassitude render me indifferent to all those things which arouse my fellow-creatures. All my illusions have fled. Not one single joy is left me. Why, then, should I hesitate? One flash from this pistol, and all would be over! Oh! my daughter, the only living being that could attach me to earth, why have I forever lost you? Once more will I pronounce your name—pronounce it with my dying breath, and then bid the world adieu."

He placed his finger on the trigger, and slowly raised the pistol to his head. At this instant, either by chance, or a decree of Providence, the door opened, and two persons entered. A minute later, and Frederick Marvennes would have ceased to breathe! His first impulse was to hide the weapon, and curse those who had disturbed him in his project. He had not yet distinguished the features of the new comers, when a well-known voice exclaimed, "Fear nothing, Juliette, I perceive Mr. Marvennes."

"Maurice!" uttered Frederick.

"My visit astonishes you, Sir," said Maurice. "I certainly did not expect to see you just now," replied Frederick. "My sister and I," continued Maurice, "beg your pardon for presenting ourselves at this undue hour, without being announced, but we could not meet with a servant."

"You have done right to come," said Frederick.

"Oh, Sir, since you left Tours, we have experienced a great misfortune," exclaimed Maurice.

"What has happened?" asked Frederick.

"We have lost our father," answered Maurice, pointing to Juliette's black dress.

"Is this your sister?" asked Frederick, looking at Juliette.

"Yes, Sir," replied Maurice.

"Poor children! But what is your object in coming to Paris?" inquired Mr. Marvennes. "After the death of our father," replied Maurice, "we were left without resources. I thought of you, Sir; I recollected your kindness to me, when you were at Tours, and the invitation you gave me to apply to you, if I were ever in distress. I said to Juliette, let us go to Paris. Mr. Marvennes will procure me employment, on which we shall both be able to live. I borrowed a little money, and my sister and I left Saint-George, placing our hopes in Heaven and you."

Frederick dropped his head, and remained thoughtful. Could he abandon these poor young creatures, who implored his succour and protection? Yet he was too much bent on his dreadful project to be deterred from it even by the opportunity offered him of living for the accomplishment of a noble action. After some moments of hesitation, he replied: "If you had come to Paris a month sooner, I could have been of use to you; I would have welcomed you as my children. A month ago I was rich, but now I am as poor as yourselves."

"Is it possible!" exclaimed Maurice.

"Oh, Sir," said Juliette, encouraged by the frankness of Frederick, "why should the loss of your fortune deprive us of the happiness of living with you?"

"My daughter would be about her age," thought Frederick, while listening to her.

"Everything, I am sure," continued Juliette, "can be retrieved."

"In what way, my dear?" asked Mr. Marvennes.

"By work," replied Juliette, with that *naiveté* which characterized her; "if you liked, we would live with you in one house—yours. I and Maurice would work with all our might. We would be your children, would attend on you, would love you, do your bidding; and you, in return, would protect us. Oh! I am sure that you would soon forget the loss of your fortune. How happy we should be, if you were to approve of this plan! Oh, Sir, do not refuse us."

"Oh, no, do not, I implore you," added Maurice.

A terrible combat had commenced in the breast of Frederick Marvennes.

"It is so sweet to live when one loves!" whispered the angelic smile of Juliette.

"Why hesitate?" replied the voice of his recollections.

Made irresolute by the influence of these two sentiments, Frederick could not reply.

Juliette became more eloquent in her pleading. "Oh! I could love you as a father," said she, "as I would have loved my own, had I been happy enough to know him."

"What!" exclaimed Frederick, astonished, "are you not the daughter of Jérôme Ballue? Maurice had always given me to believe you were."

"Like myself," replied Maurice, "Juliette is a foundling. She was picked up in Paris by my father, on the steps of Saint Roch's."

"On the steps of Saint Roch's!" exclaimed Frederick, struck with a sudden thought. "In what year?"

"In 1816," answered Maurice.

"In 1816!" repeated Frederick, in the greatest agitation. "Had not Juliette a medallion round her neck?"

"Yes," replied Maurice, "a portrait."

"Is it still in your possession?" asked Frederick.

"Oh! it has never quitted me," replied Juliette; "every day I cover it with kisses, Sir?"

"You must show me this portrait," said Frederick, trembling with emotion. "Let me see it; let me see it."

"There," said Juliette, putting it into his hands.

Frederick seized it, cast his eyes on it, and uttered a cry of joy:

"My daughter! Juliette, you are my daughter!" sobbed Frederick.

"You my father!" exclaimed Juliette, throwing herself into his arms. "Oh! I ought to have known it by the love I felt for you!"

"Can I believe my ears!" exclaimed Maurice.

"How lucky it was we came to Paris!"

"Oh! Heaven!" cried Frederick; "forgive me for having doubted of your bounty! I have blasphemed your name! Oh! pardon me! Come, Juliette, come to the arms of your father, and let him look upon you. This has been my hope for sixteen years. Oh! what happiness to hold within my arms the child I thought was lost to me forever! Oh! never,—never shall you leave me more!"

"No, never, dearest father!" sobbed Juliette, clinging round his neck.

"Poor child! you are cold," said Frederick; "your journey has fatigued you. Your hands are numbed; let them warm in mine."

"Do not weep, father," said Juliette.

"These tears relieve me," said her father. "Do not check them. I feel as if my heart was lightened of a crushing load of bitterness. Oh! how well you acted, Maurice, in coming to Paris! Like a madman, I was about to die, without having embraced my child—an angel sent by Heaven to save her father. Oh! now I wish to live. I feel rich, strong, and happy. Wealth, happiness, strength,—all are contained in a daughter's kiss! Who now dares say that I am ruined?"

"Then, now," said Maurice, "there is no longer any obstacle to Juliette's plan."

"No, Maurice, none. Henceforth we will live and work together," replied Frederick. "I will cast aside these sumptuous clothes, which, like Dejanira's tunic, have poisoned all my being. I will not longer be Frederick Marvennes, the idler and man of fashion. I will turn workman, and earn my daily bread with courage. I will dig, or break stones, if necessary. Come, let us leave this house. All my misery is left here. This day does a new life commence for me."

X.

THE GARRET

AS soon as Frederick was installed in his new abode, he began to think of the perils of his situation. What was he to do with his daughter and Maurice? His resources were not sufficient to protect them long from the attacks of poverty. Eleanor's predictions filled his mind; and he grew pale when he thought that his daughter would, perhaps, have to undergo privation. For himself, he did not dread poverty. He would have blessed his present lot, had he not feared to see his daughter want; for he felt young again, and full of hope and ardour. He had turned from death, and wished to live. All those feelings which animate man had turned to his soul, so long deprived of every pure emotion. Like a traveller, lost in a burning desert of sand, he had, at last, discovered a beautiful oasis.

The sentiment of his duties, however, did not allow him to enjoy any long repose. He soon began, therefore, to make use of the brilliant education he had received, and, by devoting himself to teaching, he succeeded beyond his expectations. Having given publicity to his intentions, he soon found himself surrounded by pupils.

Juliette, on her side, too, was not inactive. Although her father insisted that the care of the household was enough for her, she employed her leisure time by taking in needlework.

By a singular coincidence, she met, at the house of a lady for whom she worked, with the niece of Mr. Delaborde. The two young girls soon renewed their acquaintance. As soon as they were alone, Lucie questioned Miss Marvennes about Maurice; and Juliette gave so eloquent a description of his sadness and despondency, that Lucie accompanied her home, with the laudable design of consoling the poor artist. Unfortunately, Maurice, who certainly did not expect such a visit, was not at home; but Juliette induced Lucie to wait.

"Maurice will soon return," said Juliette. "He will be so happy to see you!"

"Your brother has told you, then, that he loved me?" remarked Miss Delaborde.

"Oh! no. He has not *told* me, but I have guessed as much," said Juliette, smiling. "It was not very difficult to discover, for I have often found him in ecstasy, before a portrait of you, that he has painted from memory. He spends hours in looking at, and speaking to it."

"Can you show me this portrait?" said Miss Delaborde.

"Oh, certainly," replied Juliette. "Look there; there it is, hidden under that cloth."

"Oh, how like me!" exclaimed Lucie, visibly moved. "How well he has remembered my features," added she, in a low tone.

"Several persons," said Juliette, "have wanted to buy it, but he would never sell it, notwithstanding the high prices he has been offered."

"Poor Maurice!" sighed Lucie.

"Oh! he is not much to be pitied, if you love him," exclaimed Juliette, with charming *naiveté*.

Lucie looked down in great confusion.

"Have I offended you, Miss Delaborde?" asked Juliette, much surprised. "If I have, pray pardon me."

"No, you have not offended me at all. You have only reminded me of my station," replied Lucie. "I was already dreaming that I was poor, free, and as happy as yourself. I forgot—"

"Are not rich people allowed to love, then?" asked Juliette.

"Why do you address me so singular a question?" replied Lucie.

"Because you were just now wishing you were poor, on account, no doubt, of my brother," replied Juliette.

"You are right. The rich, whose brilliant existence is so much envied, are condemned to feel but for those whom fortune places high in society's scale. Those, whom chance has made poor, ought to inspire us with nothing but indifference and contempt," said Lucie, bitterly.

"Riches would render me very unhappy, then, were I obliged to submit to such conditions," remarked Juliette; "for I love everybody—my father, Maurice, and—and—" Juliette, in her turn, looked down and blushed.

"Oh! oh! there's an *and*, is there? But, do you mistrust me, Juliette?" said Lucie. "I think that I have the right to ask you your secret, since you know mine."

"Well, then," said Juliette, "I think I love a young man who lives opposite us. But I am not so ambitious as my brother. Mr. Paul, that is his name, is poor; as poor as I am. He has assured me that he only earns a hundred francs a month, in a lawyer's office. There, Miss Lucie, that is my secret."

At this moment, somebody knocked at the door. "Here is my brother," said Juliette; "you must give him a surprise. Get into this closet."

As soon as Lucie had disappeared, Juliette opened the door, and Maurice entered. He was sad and thoughtful. He took from off his picture the cloth thrown over it to protect it from the dust, sat down, and began to prepare his palette, for Maurice, it must be known, worked most assiduously. He no longer merely daubed his canvass with colours, but each of his productions gave proof of great application and thought. The picture on which he was then working was destined for the exhibition at the Louvre. In consequence, he only uncovered it in his moments of inspiration.

Lucie silently left her hiding-place, and surprised the young artist as he sat, in an attitude of great melancholy, before his picture. With his elbow resting on his knee, and his head in his right hand, he appeared wholly absorbed by his thoughts. Lucie approached him gently, and whispered in his ear: "Hope and courage, Maurice!"

XI.

THE COUSINS

MAURICE gently rose from his seat, passed his hand over his face, as if he wished to see whether he were dreaming, and then cried out:—"Lucie, is it really you I see, or is it some kind fairy that is come to bring me hope and courage?"

Juliette was greatly amused at her brother's astonishment; and Lucie, as soon as she had surmounted her emotion, which it cost her an effort to do, replied:—

"Unfortunately, Maurice, I am not a fairy; for, if I were, with a stroke of my wand, would I change this room into a magnificent palace, of which I would make you the prince. But, alas! I am only a poor mortal, unable to pay the gratitude I owe you."

"Oh, do not speak thus, Lucie," exclaimed Maurice; "your presence procures me joy enough to wipe away years of suffering. How shall I express my thanks to you?"

"By not suspecting those who love you, Maurice, and, above all, by not despairing of the future," replied Lucie. "Juliette, Sir, has informed me of your proceedings."

"Scold him well," said Miss Marvennes. "He will listen to you more than he does to me."

"It was wrong, very wrong of you, Maurice, thus to give way," continued Lucie.

"Separated as I was from you, Lucie," said Maurice, "how could I escape despondency! Your absence made me lose both energy and courage. Doubt seized hold of me, and I imagined that you were lost to me forever. But now that Providence has again thrown me in your way, my hopes will return stronger than ever."

"So, Sir, you suspected me of violating, in the midst of frivolous pleasures, the vows I had pledged so solemnly!" again began Lucie.

"No, Lucie, I did not suspect you, but I was afraid, I own, lest you should yield to the persecution of your family," said Maurice.

"I have had plenty to endure, I can assure you," said Lucie. "My dear cousin, my aunt, and Baron Barcas have spared me neither torments nor humiliations. They, no doubt, thought, by continual attacks, to triumph over my resistance; they succeeded, however, but in making me still more inflexible; yet, I willingly underwent the trials imposed on me by Heaven, because I knew that you, Maurice, were struggling with adversity."

"Oh! Lucie," exclaimed Maurice, "why have I not followed your example, instead of passing my time in regret and idle thoughts. But I promise never to do so again."

"Hope, Maurice, and I am sure that you will some day occupy a high position in your profession," said Lucie.

"Oh! that your prediction may be realized," murmured the young artist.

At this instant, a man's step was heard on the landing. The noise approached, and a minute afterwards a voice was heard to say, in a low tone: "Miss Juliette, are you alone?"

Lucie shuddered.

"Can it be he?" she murmured.

"Oh! fear nothing," said Juliette, "it is only Mr. Paul."

Juliette opened the door, and Mr. Paul entered. On seeing him, Maurice and Lucie uttered simultaneously a cry of surprise. Mr. Paul himself appeared astonished, and was vexed at having entered, but seeing, since he was recognised, that retreat would be ridiculous, he tried to look at ease.

"Maurice—Miss Delaborde," said Juliette, "permit me to introduce to you Mr. Paul."

"Since when is my cousin Albert's name Paul?" asked Lucie, ironically.

Juliette turned as white as death: "Your cousin——He?" exclaimed she.

"Himself," answered Lucie.

"Oh! Heaven!" gasped Juliette, falling into a chair.

"Sir!" said Maurice, clenching his fists, and advancing towards Albert, "be good enough to acquaint me with the object of your visit."

"Certainly," replied Albert, embarrassed, "I came to—to—fetch my cousin."

"It is false, Sir," indignantly exclaimed Lucie.

"As amiable as usual," said Albert, trying to smile.

"Yes, Sir," continued Lucie, "it is false."

"Prove it," said her cousin, with effrontery.

"Do not call dissimulation to your aid," said Lucie; "by so doing, you aggravate your faults. The name that you have taken, this incognito in which you have disguised yourself, both show that your object in coming here was far from being honourable. You have been occupying your leisure moments in deceiving a young and inexperienced girl. Shame on you, Sir. By unmasking you, I have, however, saved her from danger."

Juliette, yielding to the violence of her emotion, covered her face with her hands, and burst into tears.

"My dear cousin," said Albert, affecting great calmness, "it does not become you to assume such airs of virtue, at a moment when I find you closeted with your paramour."

"Oh, Sir!" replied Lucie, looking down and blushing at this outrage.

The tables were turned, Albert's sarcasm had fallen like a thunder-bolt on his cousin, who, in her solicitude for Juliette, had forgotten the equivocal position in which she herself stood.

"Do not blush, my dear cousin," continued Albert, "your passion does you honour, for, in order to see the object of it, you have had to ascend as high as a fifth story."

At this abortive, yet gross attempt at wit, Lucie smiled disdainfully.

"Oh! it's a pretty story, and is worth telling again," continued Albert, in the same strain.

"It would be, Sir, a shameful calumny!" cried Maurice, scarcely able to contain himself. "And did you but possess the slightest degree of honour, Sir, you would shrink from slandering so pure a creature, who——"

"Who gives you a rendezvous," added Albert.

"Scoundrel!" thundered Maurice, about to precipitate himself on Albert.

Juliette rushed towards her brother.

"No, Maurice," she exclaimed, "I beseech you, do not strike him."

"Leave! Sir, leave the house directly!" cried Maurice, menacing Albert. "Do not pollute our abode any longer by your presence."

"Oh! I'll revenge myself," muttered Albert, opening the door.

His departure was followed by a dead silence. They were all three agitated by painful emotions. The first to speak was Maurice, who said: "Poor girl! you loved him then, Juliette?"

A flood of tears was his sister's only reply.

"Do not weep, Juliette, my cousin is not worth regretting," said Lucie.

"Oh!" murmured Juliette, "I am weeping for my faults, Miss Lucie. If I had not encouraged Mr. Albert, the scene we have just witnessed would not have taken place."

"I think, my dear friends," said Miss Delaborde, placing her hands in Juliette's, "that I had better leave you now to anticipate the calumnies of my cousin."

"Yes, leave," said Maurice, in a voice that bespoke both resignation and despair; "bid me an eternal adieu. You have been far too long a time the victim of your generosity; and I, who would willingly give every drop of my blood to spare you a single moment's pain, will not owe my happiness to misery. No, I will no longer aspire to the hand of one so beautiful and rich. In spirit alone must we be united; adieu!"

"Adieu for the present, Maurice, but we shall soon meet again," said Lucie.

She hurried away, and the rustling of her dress was still heard on the staircase, when Mr. Marvennes entered. On embracing his daughter, he felt that her face was wet with tears.

"Juliette," said he, "what has happened during my absence? you have been weeping."

Maurice implored his sister, by signs, not to acquaint Mr. Marvennes with the cause of her trouble. Juliette therefore remained silent.

"Why do you not answer me?" said Frederick, in a tone of gentle reproach. "Are you afraid I should scold you? This would be the first time."

"Well, yes," said Juliette, who could not tell a falsehood, "I have been weeping, while thinking of my mother!"

On hearing this, the features of Mr. Marvennes violently contracted.

"Poor girl!" murmured he, "she suffers. But, whatever it may cost her, she must never learn her mother's name!"

XII.

SEDUCTION

WHEN Baron Barcas came to Paris with Mr. Delaborde, he had in his possession two hundred thousand francs. He immediately hired a house, engaged servants, and set up a carriage, on the panels of which his arms were painted—a sword, surrounded by laurels, with the following motto: *Protegit virtutem*. Thanks to this heraldic display, to his cunning, and gentlemanly manners, the Baron passed for a man of noble birth, and was, in consequence, received in the most aristocratic houses of the capital.

By his example and advice, he had perverted the mind of Albert Delaborde, whom he hoped to make his dupe. Under such encouragement, Albert gave full sway to his inclinations. If debauchery had not exterminated in him all sense of morality, Juliette would have saved him from the abyss of crime towards which the Baron was conducting him. As he had been baffled in his projects by his untoward meeting with his cousin, he thought that the Baron would be able to aid him in his design. In consequence, he directed his steps towards the house of his friend, whom he found, as he wished, alone.

"What miracle brings you here, Albert?" cried the Baron, in a tone of gratified surprise.

"I merit your reproaches," replied Albert. "It is a fortnight since I have had the pleasure of seeing you."

"And what is the meaning of your long absence?" inquired the Baron.

"My dear friend, I'm afraid you will laugh at me; but the fact is, I'm in love," replied Albert.

"In love!" cried the Baron, smiling. "And with whom? With an actress, a dancer, or a dress-maker?"

"No," replied Albert. "With a woman."

"Whew!" whistled the Baron. "It appears, then, that it is a serious case. Let's hear. Some haughty siren, I suppose, that allows you to sigh to every tune before deigning to warble with you; eh?"

"No, Baron, you are out again," replied Albert. "I am tired of silk and lace. It's—"

"Peasant girl," added the Baron! "Simple, virtuous, and poor, I suppose; three titles that sound badly to my ears. Beware, Albert, of roses in a garret: they are surrounded by thorns. It's a fine thing, indeed, to seduce the daughter of a poor man, and then to have after you five or six savages, father and brothers, who howl and bite like mad dogs!"

"A truce with your preaching!" replied Albert; "I want Juliette; and, what's more, I'll have her. Besides," added he, with a cynical expression which would have shocked any other man but Baron Barcas, "I satisfy my love and vengeance at the same time."

"Your vengeance?" said the Baron, inquiringly.

"Yes, Juliette is this Maurice's sister," replied Albert.

"Indeed!" exclaimed the Baron.

"And Maurice is my cousin's lover. See how all are linked together!"

"Is this true?" asked the Baron.

"Perfectly," replied Albert. "I met my cousin in a garret, in which were Maurice, Juliette, and myself. A strange adventure, was it not?"

"You must not lose a moment, Albert," said the Baron. "Go instantly and acquaint Mr. Delaborde with his niece's conduct. Do not spare her. She is for trying to set him against you."

"I am aware of it," said Albert. "My father, thanks to her, is very severe towards me; he never replies to my demands for money, and I am forced to borrow at enormous interest. Upon my word, I don't know what my father means to do with his money!"

"It will come to you sooner or later," remarked the Baron, with a smile.

"Yes, but I don't know when," muttered Albert.

"Tomorrow, perhaps," whispered the Baron. "Your father may die suddenly; who knows? and then——why, you would inherit a million. Oh! what a life for you! No more trouble, no more obstacles thrown between you and your pleasures!"

"Oh! Baron, hold your tongue, if you wish me to wait," exclaimed Albert, greatly agitated.

"I am happier than you," remarked the Baron, "for I expect nothing."

"Am I not your friend?" asked Albert. "Were I to come into my property tomorrow, tomorrow you should be as rich as I."

"This generosity, Albert——" began the Baron.

"Do not thank me too soon," added Albert. "I should simply acquit a debt I owe you for the immense services you have done me."

"Time would change your way of thinking," rejoined the Baron.

"Friendship, founded on sympathy in tastes and character, is lasting, Baron," said Albert. "What I like in you above all is the jolly companion seeking in life for the pleasures it can give, and ridiculing everything. I am determined to laugh and amuse myself till the last moment."

"But, Albert, do you care much about this girl?" asked Baron Barcas.

"Certainly I do," replied Albert. "I never before so ardently desired the possession of a woman. I know very well that I shall succeed, but it will be with great difficulty. Juliette will no longer receive my visits, now she knows who I am. I had made her believe that I was a poor clerk. The only way to obtain her is by a forced elopement."

"It's a bad and ridiculous way," remarked the Baron. "You must have studied her character. Is she fond of finery?"

"No," replied Albert.

"Proud?"

"No."

"Idle?"

"No."

"Ambitious?"

"No."

"She is an angel, then?"

"I think she is."

"If she has no bad passions, she must be attacked through her sensibility. Has she still her parents?" inquired the Baron.

"Yes," replied Albert. "She lives with her father and Maurice. Oh! I must not forget to tell you a circumstance which appeared to me very singular.

She showed me one day a portrait, her mother's, which strikingly resembled Mrs. Delaborde."

"Was it not a small miniature round her neck?" asked the Baron, after reflecting for an instant, and as if struck with a sudden idea. "

Yes."

"Well, then, young man," said the Baron, "it is now five o'clock. Tomorrow, at the same hour, you shall hold Miss Juliette in your arms."

"You are joking, Baron," exclaimed Albert.

"Not in the least."

"But how will you succeed?" inquired Albert. "It will be impossible, unless you possess a talisman which is irresistible to woman."

"No questions, if you please; but only place faith in my promises," said the Baron.

"I will, Baron. Faith alone is able to save us."

"Is your house in the rue Amsterdam occupied? oh, I forgot—Lydia!"

"She is no longer there. We have quarrelled. She was ruining me," said Albert.

"Well, in that case," added the Baron, "be there tomorrow at five o'clock, and your goddess shall appear."

"Baron, you are a second Cagliostro."

"Ah, by-the-bye, the address of this angel?"

"There it is," said Albert; "and here is the key of my little room directly opposite, whence you will be better able to watch her movements. Goodbye, Baron; I place all my hopes in you."

"Ah! ah! Mr. Marvennes," murmured the Baron, as Albert was going out, "so, I shall, at last, be revenged on you. The honour of your daughter shall pay for your proceedings at Tours."

The next day, after ascertaining that Mr. Marvennes and Maurice were both out, Baron Barcas knocked at their lodgings. Thinking that it was Maurice or her father, Juliette hastened to open the door; but at the sight of a stranger, she experienced a slight degree of fear.

"Albert's taste is not bad," thought the Baron contemplating his victim.

"What is your business, Sir?" said Juliette, trembling.

"I wish to speak to you for an instant, Ma'am," replied Baron Barcas.

"But, Sir, I don't know——"

"Whether you ought to grant what I ask," said the Baron, interrupting her. "One word will end your hesitation and calm your fear. I come from your mother."

"From my mother? Do you, then, know my mother, Sir?" said Juliette, approaching her visitor.

"Yes, and she has begged me to take you to her directly," answered the Baron.

"And shall I be able to embrace her? Oh! Heaven, what happiness!" exclaimed Juliette.

"She is waiting for you; come," continued the Baron.

"I thought—I thought my mother was at London. I was always told so," said Juliette.

"You have been deceived, my dear young lady. She has never quitted France, and she is, at this moment, in Paris," replied the Baron.

"What! in Paris, close to me?" inquired Juliette.

"Close to you, as you will see in a few minutes," replied the Baron.

"Oh! Sir, were I to listen but to my heart, I should go with you immediately to see her, but, now I recollect, my father has forbidden me ever to attempt discovering who she is," said Juliette.

"What! Mr. Marvennes?" said the Baron.

"Yes, Sir."

"He cannot forgive her for having abandoned you, at a time when she was in great distress," said the Baron.

"What! Sir, do you know that—"

"That you were found on the steps of St. Roch's?" interrupted the Baron. "Yes, and that you had a small portrait round your neck."

"That is, true," said Juliette. "Yet I do not accuse my mother. I love her as much as if I had passed my whole life by her side. Every night I pronounce her sacred name in my prayers, and embrace her portrait."

"Your mother loves you as much as you love her," said the Baron. "I shall not be able to return to her without you, for she would die of grief, on learning that you had refused to see her."

"Oh, Heaven! what shall I do!" said Juliette.

"Why do you hesitate? Mr. Marvennes will not know the motive of your absence."

"But he would be uneasy," replied Juliette.

"Spare him all uneasiness, by leaving a few words. Here is a pen," said the Baron, placing paper and ink before her.

"No: I should do wrong," murmured Juliette.

"You would be back in an hour," said the Baron.

Juliette took the pen, and wrote a few lines to her father.

"Now, said the Baron, "make haste; we have no time to lose."

His carriage was waiting in the street; he handed Juliette into it, and bade the coachman drive at full speed. In a quarter of an hour, they arrived at the rue Amsterdam. The equipage stopped before a small house, the shutters of which were all closed. It seemed uninhabited. The gates were thrown open, and the carriage entered a little court-yard. Baron Barcas and Juliette alighted, ascended a flight of steps, and, after passing through the hall, entered a drawing-room. The Baron there begged his lovely victim to wait an instant for her mother. When alone, Juliette felt afraid. The silence of that mysterious house terrified her. She began to reflect on what she had done, and regretted having yielded to the solicitations of the Baron. She became uneasy, and thought it strange that her mother had not received her on her arrival. She was reflecting thus, when she heard the sound of steps approaching the apartment. Her suspicious vanished at the anticipated joy of embracing her mother. Her emotion was so great, that she could hardly stand. Her heart beat so quickly, that it seemed ready to burst through her delicate breast. At last the door opened, and Albert Delaborde appeared. Juliette remained rooted to the ground. Albert advanced towards her.

"Good day, my charming Juliette," said he.

"Oh, Heaven! where am I?" exclaimed the affrighted girl.

"Oh, don't alarm yourself, my pretty one; you are in no danger whatever. Here, Juliette, if you like, we can be happy, far from everyone, in each other's love," said Albert.

"How can you dare speak thus, Sir, after laying such a snare for me; and, after using my mother's name, to bring me here?" said Juliette, in a voice of indignation.

Albert changed his manner. "Am I, then," he began, "very guilty, Madam, for having employed an innocent *ruse* to extricate you from a position which could not be suited to your taste? Such treasures of grace and beauty as you possess ought not be buried in obscure poverty——"

"Spare me words, Sir, that I do not wish to hear," said Juliette. "I am very happy, with my father: I have no wish for riches. Was it your intention, by enticing me here, to dazzle me with your brilliant offers?"

"No, Juliette, I only wished to know if you would, some day, partake of my affection, of my love," replied Albert.

"You have deceived me, Sir, and I shall never love you," said Juliette.

"Never!" exclaimed Albert, unable to contain himself. "Juliette, you have pronounced your condemnation."

"What do I hear?" shrieked the terrified girl.

"You are, I say, in my power, and I am in a position to take by force the love you have refused me," said Albert.

"Oh! in the name of everything you hold most dear," exclaimed Juliette, "let me leave this house; you cannot, surely, mean what you have said: you have merely wished to frighten me, to punish me. I was wrong, I own, for saying that I would never love you: perhaps, some day, I shall love, or, at least, esteem you. But, oh! let me go; in the name of Heaven, let me leave this house. My father is waiting for me; he will be uneasy at my absence. Oh! let me go."

"How lovely you are now!" exclaimed Albert, whose eyes seemed to drink the tears that streamed down Juliette's cheeks.

"Oh, Heaven!" shrieked Juliette. "Save me!"

With a cry of despair the young girl sprang towards the door, but Albert stopped her, seized her in his arms, and pressed her to his bosom. Juliette tried to extricate herself from the grasp that encircled her like a chain of iron. She struggled for a few instants, but struggled in vain. Being at last entirely overcome, she fainted.

"She is mine! mine!" exclaimed Albert Delaborde, with an expression of countenance impossible to describe.

To complete this picture, the diabolical face of Baron Barcas appeared at the further end of the apartment.

XIII.

THE UNNATURAL MOTHER

AT ten miles from Paris, near the village of Chenevières, is to be seen a country seat, situated in a most delightful spot. The house is built at the foot of a hill; in front, there is a large and beautiful meadow, bordering one side of which is a wood, that stretches as far as the left side of the Marne. A short time since, this estate, called Chenevières Hall, on account of its proximity to the village of that name, had been bought by Mr. Delaborde, who used to spend to summer there. In the month of July, 1835, Mr. Delaborde was compelled, against his will, to go to Paris, on business of importance, and his wife's presence was also required there. Lucie accompanied them, because she did not choose to remain alone with her cousin.

A week after the infamous action of which he had been guilty, Albert Delaborde was dining with his friends, in a small apartment of the mansion, which resounded with the noisy laughter excited by the jokes of Baron Barcas. Two old acquaintances were also among the guests—Theodore, the melodramatic author, and Saint Phar, the poet. They were all greatly animated by the wines supplied from Mr. Delaborde's cellar, and were reasoning, or rather holding a rambling conversation, on anything and everything; talking, at the same time, of women, horses, poetry, theatres, and financial operations, and confounding all in their frivolous talk.

It was an exceedingly hot day, and the air was heavy with electricity. The thunder roared above the heads of those debauched men, in whose infernal revelry the voice of Heaven itself was drowned. To breathe more freely, Albert left the table, and placed himself at the open window. He had hardly risen, when an awful flash of lightning threw the entire heavens into a blaze, and a formidable, lugubrious sound filled the air. Albert appeared greatly terrified. Pale and aghast, he staggered from the window; a shivering seized him, and he fell motionless into his chair. One would have thought that he had been struck by lightning.

The storm was extremely violent; it rained in torrents. Theodore closed the windows; and Albert's terror became good food for the laughter of his friends.

"Do not laugh," said he, seized with a nervous trembling; "I have seen——"

"Well," they all cried, "what have you seen?"

"The seven-headed hydra of the Apocalypse?" asked the Baron.

"Or the hand writing on the wall?" said Saint-Phar.

"Ha, ha! The *Mene, Tekel, Upharsin*, of Belshazzar?" added Theodore.

"Or a wild beast?" said, in his turn, the Viscount Junior, who thought that he must, as a Viscount, say something.

In spite of all this joking, Albert remained motionless. What he had seen at the window had penetrated him with horror.

By the light of that terrible flash of lightning, he had perceived, in the midst of the field, a woman, whose eyes were raised, and her arms extended, towards heaven. At the moment the thunder pealed, this woman had fallen to the ground. "Dead! dead!" murmured Albert. "While she was weeping, and despair was driving her to madness, I was spending my time in revelry! Oh! 'twas I who merited her fate!"

"Have you finished your soliloquy?" said Saint-Phar.

The laughter recommenced. Pressed by their questions, Albert murmured the name of Juliette in the ear of the Baron.

"Why, Albert, you are as good as a play," said the latter. "What do you think, gentleman? You must excuse him on account of his age, but Albert's conscience is troubled by remorse."

These words were welcomed with a general shout of derision.

"What crime has he committed?" asked Theodore.

"Oh! a slight peccadillo—the most innocent thing imaginable. He deigned to throw his eyes on a country girl," replied the Baron.

"Oh! let us hear," said they all. "It must be amusing."

"A few words will suffice," continued the Baron. "This young girl, thinking one day, that she was about to embrace—her mother, fell, somehow or other, into the arms of Albert instead."

The laughter now was louder than ever.

"You must not believe in the fidelity and attachment of woman, my dear Albert," continued the Baron; "Juliette will not come to look after you here. She has already forgotten you, or filled your place."

"You are, perhaps, right, Baron," replied Albert, trying to drive away the phantom that pursued him. "Theodore, pass the wine." Albert filled himself a bumper, and drank it to the last drop. But suddenly rising from his seat, he exclaimed: "Hell itself is tracking me."

"Are you mad?" inquired Saint-Phar.

"It is no vision this time! Look, look!" cried Albert, pointing to the door.

They all turned round, and became dumb with amazement. They perceived in the doorway a young girl, whose aspect would have moved to pity the most insensible hearts. She was drenched to the skin with rain. The tears, which were falling abundantly down her pale, wan cheeks, mingled with the water that dripped from her garments. She seemed worn out with grief, and her attitude bespoke the most poignant anguish. Her head drooped on her bosom, and her arms hung down, as if powerless, on each side of her body, her long, fair hair flowed in disorder over her shoulders, and had it not been for the sobs which, from time to time, convulsively escaped her, she might have been taken for the statue of Grief. The sight of this unfortunate creature soon sobered the guests of Albert. Not one, however, had the courage to speak. At last, Albert advanced to meet her.

"Madam," said he, disguising his emotion in a tone of coldness, "what is your motive in coming here?"

"I have not the right, I know," replied the poor girl, in a voice rendered nearly inaudible by her sobs, "yet I am come to beseech you, on my knees, to restore me the honour you have deprived me of. For some days past, so many frightful thoughts have tortured my mind, so much horrible suffering has oppressed my heart, that I am nearly mad. I possessed the love of my father, of my brother, and the esteem and friendship of all who knew me; my existence was as happy as the day was long: you have taken all this from me; you resolutely planned to ruin me—to expose me to the contempt of the world. I had never imagined that anyone was capable of such cruelty. Heaven! what suffering has been mine. If you now abandon me, death will end my misery. Yet, no, I cannot die, my father would follow me to the grave. You see me kneeling to you. In the name of Heaven, I implore you to restore me, with honour, to my father."

The touching supplications of Juliette—for it was she—greatly affected Albert, but he immediately strove to hide the emotion which began to manifest itself in his countenance, for fear of arousing the sarcasm of his friends, whose constant care it was to ridicule the most sacred sentiments, and whose glory consisted of excelling in vice.

"Madam," coldly replied Albert, "your situation is touching—touching in the extreme, and I greatly regret that you have refused the assistance which I offered, and still offer you—"

"Money! you offered me money, Sir," said Juliette, blushing from indignation. "It is not money, it is my honour I ask you to restore."

"Really!" replied Albert, disdainfully.

"Were I alone in the world," continued Juliette, "I would have suffered in silence; you should never have seen me again; but my infamy will fall also on my father. He will end his days in shame and grief, if you do not give me your name. When I left your house, into which you had inveigled me by an infamous deception, my brain turned; the horror of my situation appeared to my mind in all its nakedness. To live was disgrace,—I therefore resolved to die. But before I could put my project into execution, Heaven, in its benignity, inspired me with the thought of seeking you, to implore from you pity for my father, whom the knowledge of his daughter's disgrace would kill. Tell me, Albert, what am I to hope?"

Albert Delaborde raised his head haughtily, and said: "You forget, Madam, who you are, and who I am."

"Great God!" exclaimed Juliette, in despair, "I have then nothing more to hope!"

"In good truth," exclaimed Baron Barcas, with a diabolical smile, "you are making a great many faces, and shedding a great many tears for nothing at all. What has happened, my dear, would have happened at some other time: so come, dry up your tears, and take a seat by me, and a glass of this good wine, which will bring back joy to your soul, and a smile to your lips."

This insult was the signal for a hundred more. Juliette was ready to sink with shame and fear. She was about to leave this hell, when one of Albert's friends stopped the way, and caught her up in his arms.

"You spare me no humiliation!" said the poor girl to Albert, while she struggled to escape from this unmanly violence.

At this moment, a servant came to say that Mrs. Delaborde had arrived.

"Gentlemen," said Albert, "I must leave you for a moment, to receive my mother."

Mrs. Delaborde did not, however, give him this trouble, as she followed close on the heels of the servant. Juliette rushed towards her as she entered.

"Madam," cried she, throwing herself at the feet of Mrs. Delaborde, "protect me! protect me!—I have been insulted—wronged."

"Who is this——girl?" inquired Mrs. Delaborde, in a tone of contempt.

"A mendicant!" hastily replied Baron Barcas.

"Oh! do not believe it, Madam," cried Juliette, "it is a falsehood. I am the victim of your son!"

There was a moment of silence. Juliette, who demanded protection from insult, and consolation in her misfortune, was offered money. She raised her head majestically, and in an accent of horror and indignation exclaimed: "May Heaven curse you, Madam! you who——"

She did not finish her sentence, for she knew that her malediction was a blasphemy. She drew back, aghast; her face became deadly pale, her eyes started from their sockets, and a terrible cry escaped her lips: a cry which inspired those who heard it with horror and affright. Mad, and not knowing whither she was going, she rushed from the room, and was soon far away from that house of iniquity. In the woman whom she had just cursed, Juliette had recognised her mother!

XIV.

ALBERT AND MAURICE

THE disappearance of Juliette caused great anxiety to her father and Maurice, who could, in no way, account for it. Juliette, as is already known, had not stated in her letter the motive of her absence. Several days were spent in searching for her; and, at last, the recollection of his rival's menace flashed across the mind of Maurice. Tormented by suspicion, he instantly called on Miss Delaborde, who acquainted him with her cousin's infamy.

"And what has become of my sister?" inquired Maurice.

"She has left me," answered Lucie, "in spite of all my endeavours to detain her. She has gone to Chenevières Hall, in the hope of awakening, in the breast of my cousin, sentiments of honour."

"Vain attempt!" said Maurice. "Albert will only deride his victim. He will show her no pity. Haughty and corrupted men, who delight in the despair of their fellow-creatures, never listen to the prayers addressed them by their victims. I, myself, will go and demand of Mr. Delaborde's son a solemn reparation for my sister: and may Heaven protect him if he refuse it!"

"Maurice," cried Lucie, "abandon this frightful resolution. A duel with my cousin would separate us forever."

"No man can escape his destiny," said Maurice, in a low tone. "It is mine to wish for the possession of a being, who is forced to fly from me as I advance. Illusions, ambition, hopes of happiness, all are gone! I liberate you from your vow, Lucie. I am no longer your affianced. My dream of love and happiness is over. Adieu!"

He hurried from the room without waiting for a reply from Lucie, who, overcome by emotion, fell, fainting into a chair. Maurice directed his steps towards Chenevières. He burnt with the desire to demand an explanation from Albert. Two o'clock struck as he entered Chenevières Hall. Albert and his friends were still at breakfast, which was now become an orgy. At the sight of Albert, that wretched young man, who was again plunged in debauchery, after committing so infamous an action, Maurice could not suppress his indignation; his cheeks became crimson, his eye flashed fire, and the hatred that had been slowly fermenting in his bosom, at last burst forth.

"There he is! there he is!" exclaimed the young man, in a voice of thunder, "revelling in debauchery, after his horrible crime. Wretch!"

"That fellow has a strange way of announcing himself!" at last, observed Baron Barcas. "Where can he have been brought up?

"Why," continued he, going towards Maurice, "if I mistake not, it is Maurice—an old acquaintance. He does not seem to have changed."

"Neither do you, Baron Barcas," replied Maurice. "Cunning still supplies in you the place of talent. But my business is not with you; it is with your pupil, Albert Delaborde."

"I am all ears, Sir," replied Albert, smiling contemptuously.

"I have but few words to say," continued Maurice, with great firmness. "The happiness of three persons, whom you have plunged in sorrow, depends upon you. I need not recall the circumstances. Not having succeeded in seducing a young girl, by presenting yourself under a false name and profession, you decoyed her away by I know not what treacherous snare, and then dishonoured her without pity. I come, therefore, to know, Sir, whether it is your intention to rescue this young creature from disgrace. Is it your intention to wipe away all trace of her shame and your own crime? Speak: is such your intention?"

"Gentlemen," said Albert, "since you have heard the accusation, you shall also hear the defence."

"Nothing can be more just," remarked Baron Barcas.

"Three years ago," continued Albert, "I was about to marry my cousin, a pretty woman, with a decent fortune. Guess who was the important person that crossed me in my love: it was this Maurice, one of my father's workmen, a fellow without a name, without a father, who gave himself romantic airs, and played the love-sick swain with my fair cousin, whom he charitably set against me through his calumnies. He played his cards so well, that Lucie was caught by his representations, and was ridiculous enough to break off a marriage, worthy of her rank, to fall in love with a mechanic. This took place at Tours. You will, perhaps, naturally imagine that, by coming to Paris, I got rid of Mr. Maurice. Quite the contrary. I discovered him again, still at his old tricks, eternally in between my cousin and me. To confess the truth, I felt vexed. In the meantime, I discovered a young girl, the adopted sister of this man. She pleased me, and I seized on her. Was it not quite fair?"

"Of course it was," said the Baron.

"You were quite right! quite right!" exclaimed all the others. "But of what does this fellow complain? He is wrong, and we absolve you."

These remarks were like so many poniards driven into the heart of Maurice.

"In all rivalship vengeance is lawful," continued Albert.

"And you, Sir," replied Maurice, whose uplifted hand brushed along the face of Albert, "have revenged yourself like a villain and a coward on a woman, on a feeble creature, who could not resist you. Shame on you, Sir!"

This language rendered Albert furious. His blood mounted to his cheeks, and, seizing a knife, he rushed on Maurice. The latter had, however, remarked his movement. He caught Albert's right arm as it was directed towards him, and flung him heavily on the floor. Maurice immediately threw himself on his adversary's breast, and, having disarmed him, held the knife, in his turn, over Albert's head. It was a terrible moment: Maurice, blinded by rage, was threatening every instant to strike his enemy, when someone hastily entered the room, rushed towards them, and seized the upraised arm of Maurice, exclaiming, in a voice of agony: "Stop, Maurice! or you will become the assassin of your brother!"

It was Mr. Delaborde. Informed of Maurice's visit to Lucie, he hastened to his country house, foreseeing what had really happened—a conflict between his two sons. On hearing the revelation made by Mr. Delaborde, Maurice threw the knife aside, and Albert rose, bursting with rage: "I must have your blood!" vociferated he, menacing Maurice: "Have you the courage to hold a sword, assassin?"

Mr. Delaborde threw himself between his two children.

"Albert," cried he, "have you not heard me? He is your brother. Do you hear? your brother!"

"Let me go, father!" screamed Albert.

"I order you to remain here," cried Mr. Delaborde. "I forbid you to touch Maurice. His death by your hands would cause you eternal punishment. The voice of Heaven, and your own conscience, would incessantly whisper in your ear these words:—'Cain! Cain! where is thy brother?'"

"I must have revenge!" roared Albert, no longer master of himself. "If you hinder our duel, father, I will drive this knife into my heart!"

At this menace, which Albert seemed ready to put into execution, everyone shuddered, and Mr. Delaborde presented a painful appearance. A cold sweat inundated his forehead; his face bore an expression of horror; and his breathing was difficult. Turning, at last, towards Maurice, he said:—"You, at least, will be more reasonable than this unworthy son. He has outraged you; yet forget your injuries. With respect to the person you hold so dear, I myself will see that justice is done to her. Do not accept this challenge. It is I, Maurice, your father, who beseech you."

Since the moment when he heard Mr. Delaborde was his father, Maurice had fallen into a sort of moral lethargy. His father's last words awoke him out of it.

"If you had seen, Sir, what took place one 9th of January, many years ago, on the road leading to Saint-George," solemnly replied Maurice, "you would not address such vain prayers to me. My mother had, no doubt, appealed to you in more touching words while she lay dying of cold and hunger on the roadside; yet, you were without pity for her. It was you, however, who had brought her to that frightful state. A stranger did what you refused to do! You will now easily understand why this name of father, generally the source of happiness and joy awakens in my heart no sentiment of tenderness or love. I know you not, Sir; I do not wish to know you, because I cannot love you."

"Maurice!" exclaimed Mr. Delaborde.

"Besides," continued Maurice, "did you not drive me, in 1832, from your house, on account of my birth? You, however, knew that I was the child of Magdalene Simon. It must, indeed, be a strong motive that forces you to acknowledge me now. Oh! you think that the life of your legitimate son is in danger; you tremble for *his* life. Tranquillize yourself; your son will kill me, as you, Sir, killed my mother twenty years ago."

The manufacturer could reply nothing to these bitter reproaches, as they fell from the wounded soul of Maurice. He stood motionless, in the middle of the room, as if his feet were nailed to the ground, suffering a thousand tortures.

"Come, gentlemen, let us be off," said Albert, making as sign to Maurice and his friends at the same time.

Everyone departed except Mr. Delaborde.

"Since they will not listen to me," said he, "there is only one means of preventing this duel; I must inform the police."

He rushed towards the door; but, at this instant, Eleanor appeared, and with a firm voice and imperious gesture, said to her husband: "Stay, Sir! stay."

XV.

PETER BLANCHARD, THE SPY

MR. DELABORDE paused.

"Do you know, Madam, what has taken place?" asked he, wildly.

"Yes, Sir!" replied his wife, coldly. "I know all."

"And you detain me!" cried he. "Let me go; you can speak to me at some other time."

"You shall not go, Sir," replied Mrs. Delaborde.

"Were I to listen to you, Madam," continued Mr. Delaborde, "I should let my children murder one another!"

"You need be under no apprehension about Albert," replied Eleanor, "for he is an expert duellist, and will return quite safe."

"But not before he has killed his adversary," exclaimed Mr. Delaborde. "No, Madam, I cannot allow this."

"I cannot conceive, Sir, the interest you take in this Maurice," said Eleanor.

"Are you ignorant that I am his father?" asked the manufacturer.

"When you turned him from your house, in 1832," replied Eleanor, "you were as much his father as you are now, I think. How was it that you were then so deficient in paternal love?"

"I acted wrongly, Madam," replied Mr. Delaborde; "but that is no reason why I should do so now.

"I warn you, Sir," said Eleanor, "that if you bring this bastard into your family, I will leave the house directly!"

"Eleanor," said Mr. Delaborde, in a tone of reproach.

"So, reflect, Sir," added his wife.

"Your past life does not give you the right to hold language like this to me, Madam," said Mr. Delaborde: "you apparently forget that my name alone saved you from disgrace."

"Still these reproaches, Sir!"

"If your daughter, Eleanor, if the child you have abandoned were presented to you, would you have the cruel courage to disown her? Reply."

"Yes," she replied, trying to appear calm, "I would disown her. I would spurn her, as I, this morning, spurned Albert's mistress, that young girl, who implored me on her knees!"

"May Heaven's malediction fall upon you, then, for you have spurned your child!" was uttered behind her, in a voice that shook the walls.

At this terrible interruption, Mrs. Delaborde turned quickly towards the door, and beheld Frederick Marvennes, who had entered just in time to hear her blasphemous declaration. She shrunk back with terror, fancying, in her trouble, that it was a spectre. She had thought that Frederick was dead; that he had not been able to survive the ruin.

Stupified by the sudden appearance of a man whom she imagined in his grave, Mrs. Delaborde passed her hand across her forehead, as if to drive away the clouds that clogged her brain, and advancing, pale and trembling, towards Frederick, said, in a voice scarcely audible: "Who are you? What is it you say?"

"I say, Madam," cried Frederick, "that you are a cruel, unnatural mother, and that I ought to have crushed you, without pity, the day when you were at my mercy. I should have spared you a crime!"

"My daughter! was it my daughter?" shrieked Mrs. Delaborde, writhing in the greatest agony of mind? "Oh! Heaven, I have killed her. She left this house raving mad. Despair will urge her to suicide! Come, Frederick, come! We shall yet find her, we shall yet have time to save our child."

Eleanor tried to leave the room, but she could scarcely stand. After having got half way across the apartment, she fell to the ground like a lump of clay.

"Is not Maurice with Juliette?" asked Mr. Marvennes.

"No," replied Mr. Delaborde, "Maurice is, perhaps, at this very moment assassinating his brother, my son Albert!"

"The infamous *roué*! may he die with my curse on him," exclaimed Eleanor, rising from the ground.

"Fatality pursues us, Madam," stoically remarked the manufacturer.

"No, not fatality," observed Mr. Marvennes, "but the hand of Heaven, which ever falls on the guilty. You are worthy of each other! Crime presided at your union. Prior to your marriage, you both had thrown your children on the world, without a guide, without support, without resources. Today you receive your punishment. The wrath of Heaven has fallen on you."

"Yet the punishment, Mr. Marvennes, ought not exceed the fault," said Mr. Delaborde, despairingly. "I have this night seen both my children heedless of my prayers, and I have not been able to separate them. Have I not already been sufficiently punished? In the name of humanity, I beseech you to hinder this fratricide; your ascendency over Maurice would enable you to do so; come: they are gone to fight in the wood. We shall perhaps arrive too late, even now."

"I have not the ascendency that you imagine, Sir," said he to Mr. Delaborde. "No power on earth could now reconcile your two sons, whom a whole world separates. Albert has been educated by yourself: your prejudices have been inculcated into his mind. Whilst planning seduction, whilst enjoying fortune and indulging in the pride it brings, he was taught by you to despise his brother, who was poor and disowned. You must now be astonished that Albert forgets his duty. Maurice, on the contrary, was brought up in the school of misfortune. He has learned there the knowledge of his rights—profound love for virtue, and hatred for wrong. By a fatal chance, he met with your son. Am I now to go and say to this young man, who is avenging his sister's honour: *You are wrong: cast aside your arms!* No, Sir, No! The long pent-up anger of those who suffer is not to be dispelled by a breath: it will, at last, burst forth to crush those who have provoked it!"

"Be more indulgent, Mr. Marvennes, I beseech you," cried Mr. Delaborde. "Pity for my children. Separate them, separate them!"

"It is our daughter whom we must first save," exclaimed Eleanor. "Oh! Frederick do not let her die, while cursing her mother!"

"Do not come near me, assassins!" cried Frederick, repelling Eleanor and her husband, whose hands, joined in supplication, touched his clothes.

At these words, they both hung down their heads, as if they had heard their last judgment, and Frederick hurried from the room.

We must here leave Eleanor and her husband together, while we make the reader acquainted with the details of the duel. The weapon chosen by Albert, and accepted by Maurice, was the sword. They set out. On arriving at a secluded spot, the Baron said: "This place will do very well;" adding, as he looked at Maurice, "it is nice and soft; the vanquished man will fall comfortably on this mossy grass."

While they were making the preparations, and settling the manner of the combat, Baron Barcas approached Albert, and said: "Do not forget the thrust I've taught you—one, two."

"Be easy, Baron, my memory is good," replied Albert.

"I wish they could stick each other," thought the Baron, who had an eye to Mr. Delaborde's fortune; "what a wonderful thrust it would be! But little Lucie would still be left. Pshaw! I would get her put into a convent, or somewhere else."

Continuing his ideal calculation, the Baron decided that grief would soon undermine the health of Mr. Delaborde; then, he would marry Eleanor, and seize on her husband's money bags. His fertile imagination had already made him a wealthy man, when Albert's harsh voice suddenly awoke him out of his golden dream.

"Are you ready, Sir?" cried Albert.

"Quite," answered Maurice.

The Baron frowned on seeing the awkward manner in which Maurice held his sword: his castle in the air vanished.

"The brute," he murmured, "will certainly be run through, but he won't do his adversary the same service."

Emile Saint-Phar, who had consented to act as Maurice's second, gave the signal. "Begin, gentlemen," he said.

Their swords crossed. Maurice acted on the defensive, while Albert attacked his adversary furiously, and tried two thrusts, which were warded off with dexterity. But at the third, Maurice was not quick enough; his arm was pierced, and his sword fell from his hand. Albert threw down his weapon. At the sight of the blood that ran abundantly from his brother's wound, he turned slightly pale. They all crowded round Maurice.

"Oh, it's nothing—nothing at all," said the Baron, picking up Albert's sword; "a mere scratch. You don't know how to use such weapons."

At this moment Frederick arrived at the place of combat. A look informed him of everything. He had also heard the Baron's unmanly observation, to which he replied, after picking up Maurice's sword: "Indeed, Sir! I should be delighted to have a proof of your own dexterity."

All the witnesses of this scene, with the exception of Maurice, seemed much surprised. It was evident that this new personage was entirely unknown to them. As to the Baron, he turned as pale as death, and replied, in a tremulous voice: "Do you wish to quarrel with me, Sir? Is it your intention to engage me in a duel?"

"No; in no duel, but in a murder," replied Frederick.

"It seems to me, Sir, that your mind—"

"Do not worry yourself on that point," interrupted Frederick, "my mind is right, my eye sure, and my wrist steady; I shall certainly kill you. Is not my language plain enough?"

"I must beg you to desist, Sir," said the Baron. "I am not accustomed to tolerate such language from any man, and much less from a man I do not know."

"You lie!" cried Frederick.

"Sir!" exclaimed the Baron.

"I say you lie!" continued Frederick.

"Tell me who you are, and what you want, Sir, or I shall take you for a madman," said the Baron.

"With the greatest pleasure," replied Frederick. "In 1816 I was proscribed, and you were an agent of the police, a spy. On your denunciation, I was thrown into prison for ten years. Your name was then Peter Blanchard."

"Enough, Sir, enough!" exclaimed the Baron, trembling with rage.

At this singular revelation, the friends of the Baron hurried from his side, with an air of undisguised contempt.

"A little later," continued Frederick, without paying any attention to the Baron's menacing attitude, "you put aside a name that you had rendered infamous, and took the title of Baron Barcas. Your object in so doing was to lead to crime a young mother, whose child you prevailed on her to let you carry off. Then, you introduced yourself, by *ruse* and falsehood, into a family that you have done nothing but cheat, and whose destruction you were meditating in order to enrich yourself with their property; and you have just succeeded in bringing about a fratricidal combat; your whole life, Sir, has been but one continual lie—a tissue of baseness, infamy, and treachery. But here you stop. Now that I have exposed you to your friends, under the name of Peter Blanchard, the spy, I mean to kill you like a dog."

"It is a I, liar," vociferated the Baron, "who will nail to your heart your own insulting words!"

He rushed on Frederick. The first duel had been but child's play in comparison with this. It lasted long, for the two adversaries were equally expert. The advantage, however, seemed to be with Frederick, who had kept his *sang-froid*, while the Baron had lost his in his transports of rage, caused by hearing his past life revealed. Everyone awaited the issue of the combat with an anxiety impossible to describe. Mr. Marvennes withstood the assault of his adversary, without moving an inch. He allowed him to spend his strength in vain efforts, and then, in his turn, pressed the Baron rather sharply.

"Your strength is failing you, my dear Sir, *you do not know how to use such weapons,*" said Frederick, making a vigorous plunge towards his adversary.

The Baron, pierced in the breast, staggered, turned round, and then fell heavily on the grass, watering it with his blood. Not one of his former friends ran to his assistance.

"Albert, have me taken home," said he with an effort.

Albert turned his back on him.

"Saint-Phar," murmured the dying man, "help."

The poet looked the other way.

"No one! no one to help me!" groaned he.

"No, not one!" cried Frederick, leaning over him.

"Not one single friend left! Die in your shame! die despised by all!—Peter Blanchard, your death must atone for your life!"

At this instant, cries of distress were heard in the wood.

"Help! help! someone is drowning," cried several persons at once, from the side of the river.

"Someone drowning?" cried Maurice, "oh, I'll run—"

"Stay, Maurice," said Mr. Marvennes, "you are wounded, you cannot go."

Saying this, he hurried away, and was soon on the bank of the Marne. Some peasants there told him they had seen a woman throw herself into the water. A horrid thought flashed across his mind. He quickly threw off his coat, and plunged into the river. He remained under water nearly two minutes; but at last he re-appeared, supporting in one hand the body of a woman, while with the other he swam towards the shore.

"Saved! she is saved!" cried everyone.

As soon as he was out of the water, Mr. Marvennes looked at the person he had rescued, as she lay cold and inanimate within his arms. It was his daughter! Terrified, he ran to the wood, placed her gently on the grass, and, kneeling by her side, tried every means to resuscitate her: all his efforts were in vain—Juliette gave no signs of life.

"Oh, God! oh, God!" cried Frederick, in a voice of agony, "my child is dead!"

"Dead!" repeated Mrs. Delaborde, who had just arrived, "who is dead?"

Eleanor nearly lost her senses at the sight which met her eyes. She wanted to throw herself on the body of her daughter, but a hand, dripping with blood, was raised, and caught her dress. On turning round, she saw Baron Barcas, who said to her, as he tried to raise himself on his elbow: "Eleanor, it is I. I am dying!"

Mrs. Delaborde fell to the ground from fright.

It was now quite dark. A storm had arisen. The wind whistled and played among the branches of the trees, as if it were a demon gloating over that horrible scene. A flight of birds darted from the other side of the river, and passed the theatre of so dark a drama as had that night been enacted there.

XVI.

THE TEMPTER

WHEN Eleanor came to her senses, no one was present to recall to her mind the events that had taken place; making a great effort, she tried to rise; and her hand, while feeling for some support, fell on the corpse of Baron Barcas, at whose side she was lying.

"Great God!" she cried, starting up frantically, "I have killed my child! I have killed my child!"

A prey to terror, with her hair dishevelled, and her clothes stained with blood, she ran across the little wood, calling for her daughter in the most lamentable tones.

At last she arrived home, overcome with fatigue and emotion.

"Gracious heaven!" cried her maid, on seeing her, "you are wounded, Madam! you are covered with blood! your dress is completely spoiled."

"Tell me, Theresa," said Mrs. Delaborde, "where is that young girl who came here this morning? What has become of her?"

"I don't know whether I ought to tell you," replied Theresa, somewhat embarrassed.

"She is dead!" screamed Eleanor.

"No, Madam, she is not dead; she has recovered, and is now in the front chamber."

"Come with me, then," said Mrs. Delaborde.

At that instant, however, Frederick entered. He was pensive, and as pale as death. He ordered the maid to withdraw; and approaching Eleanor, who looked almost petrified on seeing him, said coldly: "Where are you going, Madam?"

"To my daughter: my place is at her side," replied Eleanor.

"What!" continued Frederick, "are you not satisfied with what you have already done? You have thrown your daughter into misery, reduced her to despair, driven her to suicide, and now, by a refinement of cruelty, you wish to appear before her!"

"How dare you, Frederick, charge me with so infamous an action—the seduction of our child?" exclaimed Mrs. Delaborde. "Did you not excuse that infamous act?" inquired Frederick.

"Did you not encourage the miserable wretch who was guilty of it? You will now learn, Madam, that the evil we encourage in others always falls eventually on our own heads. We are invariably outdone by our vices, and punished for our faults. If you had shown a good example, and given good advice to Mr. Delaborde's son, you would not now have to suffer for his crimes."

"I had no power over Albert; he obeyed Baron Barcas entirely," said Eleanor.

"Baron Barcas, your vile paramour!"

"Sir!" exclaimed Eleanor.

"I can easily understand that it was good policy for you to take the part of the son, while you deceived the father. Albert was well aware that you were living in adultery with the Baron," said Frederick.

"This, Sir, is a calumny!" exclaimed Eleanor.

"How dare you deny it? His blood is still upon your forehead. You received his last kiss, his kiss of death!" cried Frederick, pointing to the blood on her face.

Eleanor shuddered with horror and disgust. "Oh! silence, Frederick, silence; do not drive me mad!" cried she.

"Poor creature!" continued Mr. Marvennes, after a moment's silence, looking with sorrowful compassion on the woman he had once so tenderly loved; "I forget your unworthy conduct, and feel moved to pity for you, when I think of the past. You were once pure and lovely. Eleanor, do you still recollect the day when forced to save my life by flight,

I took my last farewell of you? What protestations of love, what tears, what promises, what words then fell from your lips! When I held you trembling in my arms, I would rather have doubted Heaven than your sincerity. A year passed away; I came back to Paris. I had left an angel, and I found a demon. You had abandoned your child, bartered your soul, profaned your beauty, and delivered yourself up to the most abject wretch that society ever contained, to a spy, to a treacherous villain."

On hearing this, Eleanor raised her eyes, bathed in tears, towards Frederick. She did not appear to understand to whom the words *spy, treacherous villain,* applied.

"Yes, Madam," continued Frederick, "Baron Barcas was a miserable spy, a police agent under the Restoration. By hiding his baseness under a false title of nobility, he rose into notice, like so many others, through villany and intrigue."

On learning the ignoble origin of the Baron, Eleanor uttered a cry of horror.

"Great God! to what had I fallen!" she exclaimed.

"Into an abyss of stagnant filth. Oh, shame! oh, shame!" replied Frederick.

"Since there is now no more hope for me," murmured Eleanor, "death must wipe away these stains. Yet, before I die, grant me one thing, Frederick. Let me see my daughter——oh, if only for one instant!"

"You have no longer a daughter," replied Mr. Marvennes, in a voice of thunder. "Her malediction has separated you from her forever."

He left the room. Eleanor withdrew into her bed-chamber. She no sooner found herself alone than she threw herself on her bed, and was seized with the most horrible convulsions. In order to stifle her sobs, she bit, in her anguish, at the pillow of her bed.

Whether he feared Juliette would have a relapse on seeing Mrs. Delaborde, or whether he wished to adapt the punishment of the latter to the enormity of her fault, Frederick, it must be owned, had not shown sufficient indulgence towards the wretched mother who had begged so hard for permission to embrace her child; and yet he was better able than any else to judge of the sincerity of her repentance. Eleanor was no longer the same. The proud, corrupted woman had disappeared; and egotism and insensibility had melted beneath the first ray of maternal love.

Midnight had just struck. Eleanor, who had been unable to close her eyes, had waited for this hour with feverish impatience. As soon as the last stroke of the clock had fallen on her ears, she enveloped herself in a cloak, and left her room, stopping every now and then to listen. Silence reigned everywhere. She descended the stairs. To reach her daughter's chamber it was necessary to cross the court-yard. She walked over the gravel like a spirit fearing to make the least noise. Had anyone been leading her to death, she could not have trembled more. Having arrived at a flight of steps, which led to Juliette's apartment, she was compelled to cling to the balustrade for support. When on the last step, she stopped undecided, labouring under two contrary emotions, fear and love. The irresistible desire to embrace her daughter, urged her on, but then she feared to find herself in the presence of Frederick. Again she listened: nothing troubled the dead silence of the night. She then drew from her pocket a key that Theresa had given her, and placing it in the lock, stood still to listen once more. At length she opened the door. A night-lamp shed its dim light over the room. Her daughter was asleep. The slumbers of the young girl seemed agitated, for her bosom was oppressed, and her respiration difficult. Her right arm was thrown across the bed. Her hair fell in disorder over the pillow, and the paleness of her face, so altered by her suffering, vied with the sheets in whiteness. Eleanor knelt down at the bedside; and, after having addressed a fervent prayer to Heaven, she took her daughter's hand, and covered it with kisses. Juliette moved; and Mrs. Delaborde, fearing lest her daughter should awake and discover her, bent down so low that her forehead almost touched the ground.

"If she were to awake," murmured the unhappy mother, "she would spurn me as her father did!"

Juliette became agitated. She turned round in her bed, murmuring unintelligibly to herself. The words, "Mother! dear mother!" were, however, distinctly pronounced.

When Eleanor heard her daughter utter these words, she could scarcely contain her joy. Carried away by her affection, she clasped the hands of Juliette, and kissed them again and again. For years she had been deprived of those indescribable emotions, of those maternal joys, which, at that moment, penetrated to her very soul. During the twenty years in which she had partaken of the enervating pleasures of luxury and indolence, of the barren enjoyment of pride, and of the impure gratification of the senses, she had never experienced such felicity. It seemed to her that her being was renewed. She now felt all that she had lost by neglecting her duty. Her eyes remained riveted on her daughter's face, as she fell into a sort of ecstasy which made her, as it were, a spectator of the drama she had played. The following is the picture which passed before her mind.

In the corner of a garret, a poor half-clothed girl was engaged in needle-work. By her side was a cradle, over which she constantly bent. The smiles of her child gave her both strength and courage.

The day was cold. The air passed through the crevices of the door, and paralyzed the poor creature's limbs. Her benumbed fingers could no longer hold the needle with which she worked. "Good God!" she cried, as her work fell from her hands, "what have I done to be so wretched?

"I work night and day, yet I hardly earn enough to find my little Juliette bread. Oh! God, what will become of us?"

The poor girl had hardly ceased speaking when an unknown personage, whose eyes shone like two carbuncles, appeared before her. It was the demon of temptation.

"You are lovely," he whispered, "why, then, do you remain poor? Along the way you now tread, your feet are lacerated with thorns. Listen: despised by all, you will some day die of hunger; you and your child."

The young girl hung down her head and wept.

"Listen again," continued the stranger; "I am willing to save you. Quit this abode of poverty, and fly to one of riches. No longer thorns, but flowers will grow beneath your feet: sadness will be no longer yours, but pleasures without number: you will be no longer despised, but worshipped; you will be honoured like a queen, and adored like a goddess; you will shine in every circle; in the ballroom, at the theatre, and at church. There, look!"

The demon spread out upon the table a splendid dress and a magnificent casket of jewels, the sparkling of which dazzled, and completely fascinated, the poor simple work-girl. Her head turned. She already thought herself in the midst of a brilliant fête, and surrounded by admirers, who were disputing for her hand and expatiating on her beauty. The most delicious music filled the room and set in motion groups of lovely women, among whom she herself reigned triumphant. The work-girl, however, awoke from out of his delightful dream, and turned her head towards the cradle of her child. The child was not in it! She ran to the door and tried to open it. All her efforts were useless. It was in vain she called aloud, but no one came. She fell fainting into a chair, where she was engaged in a singular, formidable, unheard of struggle. The demon's temptations again fell on her ears. Such temptations!

On one side, she saw all the intoxication, all the delights, all the comforts, all the charms that wealth accords: an existence of gold and brilliancy. On the other, all the grief, all the fatigue, all the misery, all the cruel pangs of poverty: contempt, hunger, cold, and a pauper's grave.

The tempter still lingered.

After having hesitated for some time, the girl at last timidly approached the casket, took out the jewels, gazed on them for a while, and then arrayed her person in their dazzling splendour. The serpent had bitten her heart and wrapped her in its tightest coils. She trod under foot her coarse cotton dress, put on the one brought by the temper, and gazed at herself in a broken glass.

"You are lovely!" again exclaimed the stranger: "follow me."

She followed him.

At this moment, Eleanor awoke from her reverie. The spectres of the past were seen no more. She asked herself if what had just appeared had really taken place. No, she could not have yielded to such vile temptation. She could not have thus abandoned her child. Unfortunately, there was no possibility of blinding herself to the truth. But what would she not have given to be able to efface the last twenty years of her existence! to be able to live, as formerly, by the side of that angel, whose smiles then rendered her so happy!

"Happy are those mothers," she inwardly exclaimed, "who sacrifice themselves for their children. God loves, consoles, and supports them; for they find their happiness in their devotedness."

Eleanor heard four o'clock strike. Daylight began to invade the room. Fearful of being found there, she left precipitately, after having given a last kiss, and bidden farewell to her daughter, who was still sleeping.

XVII.

THE EXPIATION

A WEEK sufficed for the complete recovery of Juliette and Maurice. On the eighth day after the duel, the latter was walking about the garden, with his arm in a sling. The warmth of a July sun soon brought back all his former strength. After having traversed several walks, he directed his steps towards a delicious bower, the leaves of which cast their capricious shadows on the gravel. He was much surprised to meet Lucie there.

"I bless the chance, Miss Delaborde," he said, "that has brought me to you."

"Your frankness pleases me," replied Lucie, gaily. "But why, Sir, do you remain standing, like the god, Terminus, when there is plenty of room by my side?"

"Such familiarity, Madam," stammered out Maurice.

"Ought not to appear surprising among relations," interrupted Lucie. "You are my cousin, you know."

"Oh! say your brother. I love you as my sister," said Maurice, sitting down by the side of Miss Delaborde.

"And I love you more than a brother," replied Lucie, smiling.

Maurice's brow became sad.

"Are you going to turn melancholy now?" exclaimed Lucie. "Look at the sun, how gay it is. I certainly don't like this irresistible *penchant* of your sadness. Why don't you imitate nature? Overcast one moment with a storm, she appears, a minute after, radiant and serene."

"Life has been nothing but a tempest for me," replied Maurice, "from the day of my birth: yet I do not complain, for, have not you shone like a heavenly star of hope on my sombre horizon?"

"Hope, still, Maurice; better days will come, and they are nearer, perhaps, than you think," said Miss Delaborde.

"You are aware, Lucie, that tonight I leave this place, with Juliette and Mr. Marvennes," said Maurice.

"And will you attempt nothing towards a reconciliation between yourself and Albert?" asked Lucie.

"No, Lucie, nothing," replied Maurice. "Although I should like to do so, I do not think that any sincere affection could ever exist between us: we are separated by too wide a gulf. Albert's prejudices are too deeply rooted to admit of us ever being friends."

"Come, Sir," said Lucie, "have you never met, among these privileged classes you talk of, persons worthy of esteem and free from pride?"

"Yes, one, and only one,—yourself," replied Maurice.

"And is not that enough?" asked Lucie, laughing.

"My dear Miss Delaborde," exclaimed Maurice, seizing her hand and raising it to his burning lips, "you are everything to me!"

"Recollect," said Lucie, quickly, her bosom heaving with emotion, "that you are only to love me as your sister."

They went on with their conversation for a long time. The theme of it was love: a subject ever charming, and always new. Their hands were joined, their looks sympathetic, and their souls united. While they thus abandoned themselves to the chaste effusions of their affections, Albert Delaborde was holding a serious conversation with Mr. Marvennes. Eleanor, while sitting in her boudoir, which opened into the drawing-room, listened attentively to their conversation, on which the happiness of her daughter depended.

"You were inquiring for me?" asked Albert, as he entered the room.

"Yes, Sir," answered Mr. Marvennes, "I wish to speak to you for some instants."

"I am at your service," said Albert.

Each took a chair.

"In the first place," began Mr. Marvennes, sitting down, "you must not look upon me in the light of an irritated father, but rather in that of a friend."

This beginning greatly astonished Albert, who had expected a violent scene.

"Being your friend," continued Frederick, "you will allow me to act without ceremony, will you not?—to speak frankly—to use the language of truth—that language which a world of false show and hypocrisy calls *unbecoming*."

"I feel indebted to you, Sir, for thinking me worthy of listening to such language," replied Albert.

"Up to the present time," continued Mr. Marvennes, "you have pursued a wrong course. You have been swayed, on one hand, by the pernicious influence of your family and of Baron Barcas; and encouraged, on the other, by the elegant and frivolous world of fashion, which is both ridiculous and vicious. Thus encouraged, you plunged into a sea of wild debauchery, and threw to the wind of human folly the good seeds of your soul, its generous sentiments, and everything refined and noble that you possessed. You even raised a sacrilegious hand against your brother. All these faults, all these errors, great though they be, can yet be redeemed and wiped away, if you have the courage to make the attempt. At the age of six and twenty everything is possible. Arouse yourself, then. Cast aside your former mode of life; you have been the slave of shameful passions long enough; rule them in your turn, and master the fiery despots that have enthralled you. The aurora of your reformation will dispel the darkness of the past, and you will triumphantly leave that profound abyss, at the bottom of which you have met with nothing but bitter doubt and cruel deception."

Albert listened in silence to these eloquent words, of which he fully felt the justice. He remained for a few moments without replying; at last, he said in a low voice: "I acknowledge, Mr. Marvennes, the worth of the advice you give me, and thank you heartily for the interest you seem to take in me; but, unfortunately, your kindness comes too late. If I still had the slightest amount of strength or energy, I would begin my life afresh: I would raise a blaze, did there remain a single spark. But it is too late. The essence of life has evaporated. I am weary of life, and as weak as an old man. There is now no hope for me."

At this instant, the door opened, and Maurice and Juliette appeared. They presented a charming picture. The young girl had her hands clasped round the left arm of Maurice.

"There is the angel who will save you. The heart of Juliette contains treasures of tenderness and affection. Look! she is smiling at you. She has forgiven you," said Frederick.

"Can it be true?" exclaimed Albert, advancing towards her. "Can you pardon a wretch who insulted, and outraged you? Oh! it must be at your feet that I crave for pardon and forgetfulness of my crime."

"Rise, Sir," said Juliette, greatly affected. "I have no pardon to grant you. I love you."

"Oh! this happiness is too much!" cried Albert.

"Brother!" said Maurice advancing and offering his hand to Albert, who clasped it with affection.

"Brother! my wife!" exclaimed Albert, scarcely able to credit his felicity. "Oh! do not quit me, I shall no longer dread the temptation of evil. Thanks to you two, my life will now glide away in purity and happiness."

At this moment, Mr. Delaborde entered the room. He was accompanied by Lucie. We will not even attempt to describe his astonishment.

"What do I see?" said he, as if doubting the reality of his senses. "My children united! Who has brought about this miracle?"

"Love," replied Mr. Marvennes.

"Oh, I see everything now," replied the manufacturer. "Mr. Marvennes, how can I express to you the gratitude with which my heart is penetrated? You have proved the good genius of my family. You have repaired the evil I had done; for it was I who was the first cause of the misfortunes that have befallen us."

"Sir!" interrupted Frederick.

"Let me openly acknowledge my faults, and own the enormity of my errors," hastily replied Mr. Delaborde. "Let me ease my conscience. To the vile love of riches, to the immoderate desire of amassing wealth, I sacrifice the most sacred duties with the woman who loved me, and a son whose contempt I have incurred."

"No, no, father!" quickly interrupted Maurice, "do not think that."

"Forget the past," said he to his son, advancing towards Maurice, "it is the wish—doubt it not—of Magdalene Simon!"

The name of his mother greatly affected Maurice; he threw himself into the arms of Mr. Delaborde, and when his father had recovered from his emotion, Albert said to him: "I ask of you the hand of my cousin in marriage for my brother Maurice."

"Provided my niece is willing, I consent," answered Mr. Delaborde.

"I have been waiting for your acquiescence these four years, uncle," remarked Lucie, laughing.

"Well, then, you shall not wait a week longer," answered the happy father.

"Allow me, Sir, to present you my affianced," said Albert, taking Juliette by the hand. "Two contracts can be signed on the same day, as well as one."

"Certainly they can," said Mr. Delaborde, embracing Juliette. Frederick, from a corner of the room, contemplated, with ineffable emotion, the happy couples he had made.

"My friends," said he, coming forward, "remain forever united. The union of soul to soul accords both earthly and heavenly joys. Yesterday you were suffering, because you hated one another. Prejudice divided you. What is the meaning of the words *poor, rich, great, little?* Wherefore those distinctions? hasten towards the same object, leaning on each other? Let the most worthy lead the way. Excuse this little sermon, my dear friends. I am now an old man; I have acquired experience at my own cost. Chance has thrown me into every class of society. The world of fashion has presented to my view absurdities, vices, and pride. Among the lower classes I have witnessed despair and suffering, and have heard frightful menaces. I every day see multitudes arise, and beg of society for life and love! yet the unnatural mother remains deaf to their entreaties. 'No!' she replies, 'you shall obtain nothing, I have my own favoured few. For you, the disowned, I have nothing but contempt.'

"This state of things," continued Frederick, "will, I am convinced, some day cease. Some day, the members of this immense human family, at present separated by error, hatred, and iniquity, will be reconciled one with another, like you, my friends, at present. The sun of justice will cast its light upon the world, liberty will spread its wings, love will reign, and Satan will be vanquished. This day will come, and then you will see the fall of all those barriers that have been raised by ages of ignorance and despotism. And now, my friends, before I leave you, one more entreaty. Love one another; do good to all around you, and you will reap the benefit of it in the end."

"What!" cried Mr. Delaborde, "do you think of quitting us? Oh! I cannot allow that."

"My resolution is taken," replied Frederick, "I am going back to my pupils, whom I have neglected too long."

"Father," exclaimed Juliette, throwing her arms round Mr. Marvennes' neck, "do not leave us, you will break my heart."

"Fear nothing, my Juliette, I will often come to see you. Albert," added Frederick, "I place in your hands the guardianship of this angel."

"Nay," exclaimed Mr. Delaborde.

Frederick drew him apart, near to the place where Eleanor was listening.

"Do not try to detain me," he said, "I could not meet your wife."

At this instant a slight noise was heard from the boudoir; a groan followed, and then a stifled sob fell upon their ears.

"What's that?" cried Mr. Delaborde, greatly frightened.

Eleanor appeared, and horrified all present. Her face was livid, her features frightfully contracted, her hair dishevelled, and her dress in great disorder. Her lips were covered with foam, and her eyes rolled in their orbits; she rushed between Frederick and the door, saying: "You need not leave. Remain with those who love you. You shall see me no more. My presence would have troubled the happiness of this family; in five minutes I shall have ceased to live."

"What have you done?" exclaimed they all.

"I could not live, after being cursed by the child to whom I have given birth; this would have been too frightful. I have taken poison."

"Unhappy woman!" exclaimed Frederick.

"A surgeon! run for a surgeon!" cried Mr. Delaborde.

"It is too late," murmured Eleanor, falling on the sofa and writhing with agony.

"Mother! mother!" exclaimed Juliette, throwing herself to her bosom. "Adieu! Do not curse me. Adieu."

"Mother!" sobbed Juliette, "Do not die, live for my sake, I love and bless you."

"Great God!—can you—love—love—me—" gasped Eleanor, stopping for breath between each word. "Since—then—my child—has pardoned me—"

Frederick seized her hand. It was already nearly cold. "God will also pardon you," replied he in a solemn voice, "for you have atoned severely for your faults."

Eleanor struggled once again, and then she moved no more. The poison had done its work!

Juliette, who was leaning over her mother, no sooner felt that she had ceased to breathe, than she uttered a piercing shriek, and threw herself across her mother's corpse.

A year after these events, four persons, newly married, were assembled in prayer, around the tomb of Eleanor.

Behind them were two men, who, motionless and bareheaded, seemed plunged in deep meditation. The sight of those young beings, whose hearts, warm with love, now yearned after the cold ashes of the grave, inspired these two men with melancholy thoughts. Their eyes were fixed on the tombstone, and they were, no doubt, thinking of the vanity of worldly strife, whichever leads but to a few grains of dust, and a *Sacred to the Memory*, engraven on a slab.

Of these two men, one had been the affianced, and the other the husband of the person buried there.

THE END.

A PARTIAL LIST OF SNUGGLY BOOKS

G. ALBERT AURIER *Elsewhere and Other Stories*
CHARLES BARBARA *My Lunatic Asylum*
S. HENRY BERTHOUD *Misanthropic Tales*
LÉON BLOY *The Desperate Man*
LÉON BLOY *The Tarantulas' Parlor and Other Unkind Tales*
ÉLÉMIR BOURGES *The Twilight of the Gods*
CYRIEL BUYSSE *The Aunts*
JAMES CHAMPAGNE *Harlem Smoke*
FÉLICIEN CHAMPSAUR *The Latin Orgy*
BRENDAN CONNELL *Unofficial History of Pi Wei*
BRENDAN CONNELL *The Metapheromenoi*
RAFAELA CONTRERAS *The Turquoise Ring and Other Stories*
ADOLFO COUVE *When I Think of My Missing Head*
QUENTIN S. CRISP *Aiaigasa*
LADY DILKE *The Outcast Spirit and Other Stories*
CATHERINE DOUSTEYSSIER-KHOZE
  The Beauty of the Death Cap
ÉDOUARD DUJARDIN *Hauntings*
BERIT ELLINGSEN *Now We Can See the Moon*
ERCKMANN-CHATRIAN *A Malediction*
ALPHONSE ESQUIROS *The Enchanted Castle*
ENRIQUE GÓMEZ CARRILLO *Sentimental Stories*
EDMOND AND JULES DE GONCOURT *Manette Salomon*
REMY DE GOURMONT *From a Faraway Land*
REMY DE GOURMONT *Morose Vignettes*
GUIDO GOZZANO *Alcina and Other Stories*
GUSTAVE GUICHES *The Modesty of Sodom*
EDWARD HERON-ALLEN *The Complete Shorter Fiction*
EDWARD HERON-ALLEN *Three Ghost-Written Novels*
RHYS HUGHES *Cloud Farming in Wales*
J.-K. HUYSMANS *The Crowds of Lourdes*
J.-K. HUYSMANS *Knapsacks*
COLIN INSOLE *Valerie and Other Stories*
JUSTIN ISIS *Pleasant Tales II*

VICTOR JOLY
 The Unknown Collaborator and Other Legendary Tales
MARIE KRYSINSKA *The Path of Amour*
BERNARD LAZARE *The Mirror of Legends*
BERNARD LAZARE *The Torch-Bearers*
MAURICE LEVEL *The Shadow*
JEAN LORRAIN *Errant Vice*
JEAN LORRAIN *Fards and Poisons*
JEAN LORRAIN *Masks in the Tapestry*
JEAN LORRAIN *Monsieur de Bougrelon and Other Stories*
JEAN LORRAIN *Nightmares of an Ether-Drinker*
JEAN LORRAIN *The Soul-Drinker and Other Decadent Fantasies*
ARTHUR MACHEN *N*
ARTHUR MACHEN *Ornaments in Jade*
CAMILLE MAUCLAIR *The Frail Soul and Other Stories*
CATULLE MENDÈS *Bluebirds*
CATULLE MENDÈS *For Reading in the Bath*
CATULLE MENDÈS *Mephistophela*
ÉPHRAÏM MIKHAËL *Halyartes and Other Poems in Prose*
LUIS DE MIRANDA *Who Killed the Poet?*
OCTAVE MIRBEAU *The Death of Balzac*
CHARLES MORICE *Babels, Balloons and Innocent Eyes*
GABRIEL MOUREY *Monada*
DAMIAN MURPHY *Daughters of Apostasy*
KRISTINE ONG MUSLIM *Butterfly Dream*
CHARLES NODIER *Outlaws and Sorrows*
PHILOTHÉE O'NEDDY *The Enchanted Ring*
YARROW PAISLEY *Mendicant City*
URSULA PFLUG *Down From*
JEREMY REED *When a Girl Loves a Girl*
JEREMY REED *Bad Boys*
ADOLPHE RETTÉ *Misty Thule*
JEAN RICHEPIN *The Bull-Man and the Grasshopper*
DAVID RIX *A Blast of Hunters*
FREDERICK ROLFE (Baron Corvo) *Amico di Sandro*
JASON ROLFE *An Archive of Human Nonsense*

MARCEL SCHWOB *The Assassins and Other Stories*
MARCEL SCHWOB *Double Heart*
CHRISTIAN HEINRICH SPIESS *The Dwarf of Westerbourg*
BRIAN STABLEFORD (editor)
Decadence and Symbolism: A Showcase Anthology
BRIAN STABLEFORD (editor) *The Snuggly Satyricon*
BRIAN STABLEFORD (editor) *The Snuggly Satanicon*
BRIAN STABLEFORD *Spirits of the Vasty Deep*
COUNT ERIC STENBOCK *Love, Sleep & Dreams*
COUNT ERIC STENBOCK *Myrtle, Rue & Cypress*
COUNT ERIC STENBOCK *The Shadow of Death*
COUNT ERIC STENBOCK *Studies of Death*
MONTAGUE SUMMERS *The Bride of Christ and Other Fictions*
MONTAGUE SUMMERS *Six Ghost Stories*
GILBERT-AUGUSTIN THIERRY *The Blonde Tress and The Mask*
GILBERT-AUGUSTIN THIERRY *Reincarnation and Redemption*
DOUGLAS THOMPSON *The Fallen West*
TOADHOUSE *Gone Fishing with Samy Rosenstock*
TOADHOUSE *Living and Dying in a Mind Field*
TOADHOUSE *What Makes the Wave Break?*
LÉO TRÉZENIK *Decadent Prose Pieces*
RUGGERO VASARI *Raun*
JANE DE LA VAUDÈRE *The Demi-Sexes and The Androgynes*
JANE DE LA VAUDÈRE *The Double Star and Other Occult Fantasies*
JANE DE LA VAUDÈRE *The Mystery of Kama and Brahma's Courtesans*
JANE DE LA VAUDÈRE *The Priestesses of Mylitta*
JANE DE LA VAUDÈRE *Three Flowers and The King of Siam's Amazon*
JANE DE LA VAUDÈRE *The Witch of Ecbatana and The Virgin of Israel*
AUGUSTE VILLIERS DE L'ISLE-ADAM *Isis*
RENÉE VIVIEN AND HÉLÈNE DE ZUYLEN DE NYEVELT
Faustina and Other Stories
RENÉE VIVIEN *Lilith's Legacy*
RENÉE VIVIEN *A Woman Appeared to Me*
TERESA WILMS MONTT *In the Stillness of Marble*
TERESA WILMS MONTT *Sentimental Doubts*
KAREL VAN DE WOESTIJNE *The Dying Peasant*

www.ingramcontent.com/pod-product-compliance
Lightning Source LLC
Chambersburg PA
CBHW020255030426
42336CB00010B/783